WITHDRAWN

KESLING
modern structures

Balcony Press
Los Angeles

KESLING
modern structures

POPULARIZING MODERN DESIGN
IN SOUTHERN CALIFORNIA 1934–1962

BY PATRICK PASCAL

WITH PHOTOGRAPHS BY JULIUS SHULMAN AND DAVID SADOFSKY

Published in the United States of America 2002
Design by Fuse Design
Printed by naviçatorpress, Monrovia, California

Kesling Modern Structures ©2002 Patrick Pascal

Library of Congress Catalog Card Number: 2002103804
ISBN 1-890449-13-X

Cover: The Vanderpool house, Silverlake 1935, photo: Julius Shulman

Julius Shulman

TABLE OF CONTENTS

PREFACE by David Gebhard

ABOUT STYLE, NOT IDEOLOGY

In 1930 Paul T. Frankl, then famous for his designs of "skyscraper furniture," published a small volume, Form and Reform. In a chapter, "Style vs. Styles," he wrote, "What elevated men, in the last analysis, above the bees is the mastery and recognition of Style." And indeed the opening years of the '30s were, like the present episode of post-modernism, those of clashing views of the whys and wherefores of architecture and design. In fact, there are so many points of similarity between the early-'30s and our own day that we should feel slightly uneasy about our current scene. Architects were not only expressing strong views about style (or nonstyle) via the design of their buildings, but they were turning to the written word to defend their various allegiances. Then, as now, the conflicting views were not only within the realm of serious "High Art" architecture, but equally between the High-Arters and the populists. Matching Charles Jencks' Postmodernism with its purposeful ignoring of the common was Philip Johnson's Post Functionalism of 1931, which pitted the elite Internationalists against those lowly creatures who expressed the popular American Perpendicular (the Art Deco) style.

Today if we try to reconstruct what took place in American architecture during the decades of the '20s and '30s, we would more likely than not limit our comments to the work of Frank Lloyd Wright, Richard J. Neutra, and R. M. Schindler, and later to William Lescaze, Gregory Ain, and a few others; we would reveal how well we have been programmed to recite the canonical tale of High Art Modernism. But those who lived in the early '30s were far more sophisticated in their knowledge of history and what was occurring than we. As in our current encounter between the Postmodernists and the traditional Modernists, conflict existed between those who passionately believed that design must rely on precedent and those who expounded the New (International Stylists). In addition, an equally hot battle occurred between Internationalists and the popularizers of the Moderne—in the '20s the Perpendicular (Art Deco) Moderne and in the '30s the Streamline Moderne.

The intensity of the struggle between the High Art Modernists and the Traditionalists came close to being a religious war with far more verbiage exchanged about ethics, morality, social and political stances than about design and imagery. Lewis Mumford in an article on "The American Dwelling House," published in The American Mercury, April 1930, said that the answer to the design of the American house must "be found in the modern hospital"; but for Aldous Huxley there was nothing delightful about lolling around in a dwelling that reminded him of a dentist's office. Henry Russell Hitchcock and Philip Johnson continually emphasized the theme that the necessity of the new age was to express structure, materials, and function in the design of modern buildings. Leicester B. Holland at AIA's 68th convention in 1936 responded to such "expressive necessity":

Skin deep and valued at a pin
Is beauty such as Venus owns,
Her beauty is beneath the skin
And lies in layers on the bones.

Toward the conclusion of his remarks he commented: "A quiet chat with an anatomical convive, lolling, as it were, in his viscera, would be very difficult for me."

The Viennese pioneer Modernist Adolf Loos wrote in 1908 that ornament was crime. H. Roy Kelly, one of California's gifted Traditionalists, responded in 1929, with a tongue in cheek, that the modern movement in art and architecture was characterized by "restlessness and uncertainty leading to mayhem … and after all modern art (and architecture) and modern crime, perhaps, bear a closer relationship than some of us suspect."

Fortunately, the popularizers of Modernism in the '20s and '30s avoided much of this spiteful and vicious battle. The exponents of what we today label as Art Deco in the '20s and as Streamline Moderne in the '30s assumed a lackadaisical middle course between High Art Moderns and the Traditionalists. Their course partook of both because their interest lay essentially in design, not ideology. While they certainly hoped their designs would convey a modern view of the past, present, and future, they were involved with the question of visual languages.

The building's program, its structure, materials, and mechanical core were a means of realizing style—not a basic conditioner of style.

"It is in America," wrote Roger Gilman of the Fogg Museum at Harvard University (1936), "that this conservatively modern, which we might call transitional style, maintains itself so strongly." Gilman went on to touch upon a question that is often ignored or dismissed in architecture, that of producing designs that employ a language readable by a large audience. The popular Art Deco of the '20s and the later Streamline Moderne produced images that "appealed to the public by their air of progress and charm, yet cannot venture too far behind the public taste, for our man in the street is not so readily impressed by his architectural leaders as the European bourgeois" Gilman wrote.

Finally, there was the allure of the machine to the American middle-class, both as fact and symbol. Here again there was a decided difference between Europeans and Americans experience. Both before and after World War I the symbol of the machine in Europe remained an elite, High Art object. In America it was commonplace, accepted without fanfare or highfalutin poetic or High Art intervention. Within the American Art Deco of the '20s, the fact of the machine, via new technology, new structural forms, and new materials, was fully endorsed by the middle class. With no urgent desire to directly symbolize the machine in the design of buildings, the machine in America was seen as a means, not an end. The question in the popular mind (and in the minds of most practicing architects of the day) was what sort of attire (image) should be conveyed by a building that was to be considered modern. It was taken for granted that the latest technological advances would be incorporated into the building.

The Art Deco Perpendicular or Zigzag Moderne and the Streamline Moderne did succeed most effectively in capturing the public's imagination. Their widespread acceptance was due not only to their present adherence to the "beauty" of traditional architectural languages, but equally to their optimistic symbolism of the present and the future, and their feeling that romance, playfulness, and joy were integral ingredients of a well-designed building. The popular Moderne architects of the '20s and '30s had little or nothing to do with the perennial ideological hallmark of High Art Modern morality. Instead, as the gifted Colonial Revivalist architect Dwight James Baum wrote in 1933, the aims of an architect should be to produce buildings that evoke a respect for the past, for the new spirit of the day, and "satisfy man's love for beauty."

Those architects and designers who produced Art Deco and Streamline Moderne designs did not see themselves as advocates of a single image. Images had their subtle places; thus a typical practitioner such as the Los Angeles firm of Morgan, Walls and Clements or Holabird & Root of Chicago might find the design for an Art Deco skyscraper on one board, a concrete Spanish Churrigueresque or American Georgian stone building on another, and on still another a residence in the form of an Andalusian farmhouse. "Change is the life of style" wrote Frankl in 1930; he might have added that style (or the plurality of styles) is the result of fashion and taste. So when we look back on the popular Moderne of those decades, we must be aware that it was one among several styles, and as a style (a language) it underwent tremendous changes from the early '20s through the beginnings of the '40s. The design of a baked enamel, metal-clad dry cleaning establishment of 1939 is as different from a mid-'20s Art Deco store or office building, with its verticality and ornament, as is a typical English Tudor house of 1925 from a Queen Anne dwelling of the 1880s. The only common ingredient of '20s Art Deco Moderne and '30s Streamline Moderne is their shared sense of conveying modernity.

As was the case with the Art Deco Moderne at the end of the '20s, it was (Sheldon) Cheney who most eloquently caught the spirit of Streamline Moderne—the new popular Modernism of the years 1930–1942. He, together with his wife Martha, produced another classic volume, Art and the Machine (1936). This work, like his earlier one, was tremendously popular with the middle class and equally despised by the High Art International Style Modernists. "We live in a world of Streamline vehicles," wrote the Cheneys. "The streamline as a scientific fact is embodied in the airplane. As an esthetic mark, and a symbol of the 20th century machine-age speed, precision, and efficiency, it has been borrowed from the airplane and made to compel the eye anew, with the same flash and gleam beauty embodied in all travel and transportation machines intended for fast going."

To the horror of the evangelical High Art Modernists, the designers of streamline buildings and objects not only continued to regard design as styling, but in an act of unmitigated treachery set about borrowing both the visual language and some of the ideology of the Modern Movement. The Modernists from Le Corbusier on had written and spoken of the hygienic nature of Modernism. Then in 1930, Cheney came along and wrote of a slightly streamlined Chrysler

Imperial: "Here is a clean athletic transportation machine for the modern clean athletic body—and we should have houses to match."

The urge to employ Streamline design has, as one would expect, its own long history, reaching back into the late 19th century. But it was in the teens and early-'20s that the oval, curved, and horizontal forms that connoted speed began to enter the world of architecture and designed objects. For those whose view of history is a result of indoctrination in the Modern Movement, we immediately think of pre-World War I projects of Antonio Sant' Elia or the sketches of Eric Mendelsohn and his realized Einstein Tower at Potsdam (1919–1920). While Mendelsohn's works, including his sketches, were published in the U.S. at the beginning of the '20s, the principal source that explains why its later vigorous acceptance occurred in the world of science fiction. Jules Verne, H.G. Wells, and E.M. Forster set the stage for what was taken up by Hugo Gernsback and others in such pulp magazines as Amazing Stories (1928). In 1929 Gernsback coined the term "science fiction," and in that same year the first sciences fiction comic strip, "Buck Rogers, 25th Century" (John Dille and drawn by R.W. Colkin), appeared in newspapers across the country.

Both the High Art Modernists and the Streamline Moderne-ists openly borrowed from the imagery of transportation machines. Le Corbusier illustrated his 1922 "Towards a New Architecture" with various automobiles, ocean liners, and airplanes. With the exception of one drawing of "The Airplane of Tomorrow," none of his transportation machines was in any way streamlined; each was composed of individual parts that were intended to be read separately. The design of the characteristic automobile of the '20s consisted of autonomous parts: a grille and radiator, the hood, fenders, wheels, coach body, and often a separate luggage trunk. In a way, this was the manner in which an Art Deco, a historic-oriented design, or a High Art Modernist building of the '20s was to be experienced: an assemblage of individual parts forming the total image.

How different was the approach of those involved in promoting the universality of the streamline image. E.A. Whiting Jr., writing of the new streamline 1939 Hupmobile Skylark, summed up the difference between the '20s and '30s designs: "Many elements previously treated separately and applied here and there outside the basic shell are now either closed away or designed not to interfere with the sweep of the forms." In industrial designs the most popular form was

the aerodynamic teardrop, which came to be used for literally every object ranging from the pencil sharpener to the house trailer. The rationale behind this was simple and to the point. "Simple lines are modern," Frankl observed in 1928. "They are restful to the eye and dignify and tend to cover up the complexity of the machine age. If they do not completely do this, they at least divert our attention and allow us to feel ourselves masters of the machine." The purpose of the streamline in architecture and design was not to produce more efficient moving objects, but to symbolize the movement, and above all, conjure up visions of the future. The stage designer turned industrial designer Norman Bel Geddes captured this need for symbolism in his 1932 volume "Horizons": Today, speed is the cry of our era, and greater speed one of our goals of tomorrow."

Another irony of the relationship between the High Art Modernists and the popular Modernists—in this case the Streamline Modernists— was the emergence at the end of the '20s in America of the new profession of industrial designers, but hardly the architect/industrial designers the Bauhaus had in mind. By the early-'40s the star-studded galaxy of industrial designers enjoyed a prestige approximating that of Hollywood stars.

These designers were not attracted to monolithic principles of Modernism; for them it was the image that romantically packaged the machine, whether a child's tricycle or a fast-food roadside inn. Frankl's 1932 comment (in Machine Made Leisure) that "successful styling implies progressive restyling" certainly must have produced shudders from Alfred Barr and others associated with New York's newly founded bastion of High Art Modernism, the Museum of Modern Art.

One of the great advantages of the Streamline Moderne was its character could be established by a limited vocabulary of forms and details. Its basic form should be a volumetric container with surfaces symbolizing the machine: exposed concrete, stucco, vetrolite or Carrara glass, or baked porcelain enamel panels. With the exception of concrete, all of these materials were to be read as a surface skin that did not reveal one way or another what lay beneath. Articulating this surface and parallel to it (with no suggestion of structural depth) were horizontal window openings, horizontal bands, and often near the top a grouping of three horizontal lines. The window and framing should ideally be machine-like (metal), and the doors should give one the impression of entering a Buck Rogers rocketship. Finally, the two most telltale marks of the style-curved walls and glass brick should establish the indisputable modernity of it all.

Internally, the Streamline Moderne building was as shipshape as it was externally. Walls might be covered with plywood panels (to be read not as natural wood but as wood as a machine product) and sheets of plastic laminate used for cabinet tops and even for sections of walls, linoleum floors, and detailing of chrome bands. Amid all of this were tubular chrome chairs and tables, clocks and other bakelite objects, and in the more exuberant examples beds and couches of neon-lighted glass brick.

The Streamline Moderne was a fully established and accepted design and architectural style by the mid-'30s. It was taken up fragmentally or as a whole by the great majority of the American architectural profession. And as a group they carried it off well, for in essence it did not violate any of the cardinal principles of their Beaux-Arts training. The new popular style was not based upon a highfalutin ideology; it had nothing to do with the "silly" question of morality and architecture, and it, like other modern historic styles, was intrinsically an image. Though extremely popular with the middle class, it was not seen as the universal design solution for all buildings. In fact, it came to be used and associated in the public mind with specific building types: restaurants, bars, neighborhood theaters, service stations, dry cleaning establishments, dog and cat hospitals, medical clinics, and soft drink manufacturing plants. The ideal of a home for the American middle class during the Great Depression years was the colonial revival, with its sense of Puritanism and American nationalism. More often than not, one finds that when the Streamline Moderne was employed for single-family housing, the dwelling was built as a modern display house or used by a physician or veterinarian who wished to suggest to his community that here resided a man of science. The ideal middle class family rode in streamline autos, buses, trains, and airplanes, and they might have worked in a streamline building; but when they returned home, it was to the shelter of a white clapboard and green-shuttered Colonial Revival house.

Elements of the Streamline Moderne did, of course, penetrate far and wide. In the late-'30s, many of the PWA Moderne buildings created by or financed by the federal government exhibited curved walls, glass brick, and other ingredients of the style. And many middle class apartment buildings and single-family houses erected in the mid-and late-'30s conveyed their modernity by using elements of the style. Though supposedly repugnant to them, many of the High Art Modernists either fully embraced the mode, as was the case with Edward Durell Stone and Lescaze; or, as with Schindler and Neutra, they adroitly sampled here and there. And it can well be argued that the most impressive High Art version of the style was Frank Lloyd Wright's Administrative Offices for the Johnson Wax Co. in Racine, Wisconsin (1936–1939).

By the time of the 1939 New York World's Fair the Streamline Moderne had assumed the stance, as Reyner Banham has pointed out, of the new American style. Through the architectural firm of Harrison & Fouilhoux designed the theme of the fair—the Trylon and Perisphere—the real heroes of the fair were the designers Norman Bel Geddes, Henry Dreyfuss, Walter Dorwin Teague, and Raymond Loewy. The fair was a triumph of the Streamline Moderne, wonderfully captured in the ideal cities of Henry Dreyfuss' "Democracity" and Norman Bel Geddes' "Futurama." Here in a model form we immersed ourselves into "the city of the future," with a reality exceeding the science fiction film (Vincent Korda's 1936 set for "Things to Come") or one of Frank R. Paul's cover designs for Amazing Stories. The professed aim of the New York fair was "to portray the World of Tomorrow, and to commemorate the first inauguration of George Washington." And American architecture of the '30s and the fair beautifully captured the dualism of the past and present in the American middle class. The Colonial Revival and the national interest in the restoration of Colonial Williamsburg created the storybook linkage with early American, and the Streamline Moderne provided the vision of the future. At the fair itself this polarity was reflected in the dominant Streamline image of the future, countered by the placid lagoon of the Court of State, governed at one end by a version of Independence Hall and at the other by a doomed and porticoed Jeffersonian villa.

The Streamline Moderne as an image did not completely disappear during and after World War II, for scattered late examples were built here and there. But as a symbolic packaging it was out of fashion by 1945. After all, it, like all vigorous architectural styles, arrived on the wings of fashion and left the same way. As Paul T. Frankl said, "Successful styling implies progressive restyling," and Frankl and other designers/architects of the postwar period needed and found new symbols to express an era far different from that of the '30s.

INTRODUCTION

Few designers have achieved greatness without any formal training. Fewer still are those that reached the pinnacles of their careers during the depths of the Great Depression. William Kesling met both these challenges with designs that played a unique and important role in the development and acceptance of modern architecture in Southern California. At a critical time in its beginnings, he brought modern design within reach of the everyday home-buying public. His was a historically significant career, though brought to ruin by deception and extortion. The scandals have long since been forgotten, but his buildings and the weight of his influence on modern architecture remain.

The International Style of architecture that emerged from the Bauhaus and other European-based design schools was well suited to America's Depression-era realities. The economy of space and materials and the elimination of detail and ornamentation appealed to both the mood and the budget of cash-strapped builders. Such strident credos as "ornament = crime" expressed both a design philosophy and a social opinion of the day. The Depression heightened awareness of the Modernists' inability to deliver on the promise to provide comfortable, affordable housing. Streamline Moderne, with its curves, windows, and imagery of motion and speed, emerged as a uniquely American variety of the International Style. Having captivated the imagination of the American public, this architecture flourished for a very brief period during the mid to late thirties. In horizontal, automobile-oriented Los Angeles, Streamline design held a special attraction.

The lightweight construction and open floor plans common to the style were ideally suited to Southern California's mild climate. The growing Hollywood film community offered clients with the means and inclination to build such homes. Los Angeles' sun, lush landscape, and clients allowed Streamline design to realize the ideal of the "machine in the Garden." It was during this decade that Southern California firmly established itself as a world-class center of modern architecture.

Over a one-year period beginning in November 1935, William Kesling was far and away Los Angeles' most prolific and successful practitioner of Streamline Moderne design, breaking ground on more than twenty projects. His better-known Modernist peers such as Schindler and Neutra could not as easily desert the principles of simplicity and austerity. The unschooled Kesling was not bound by any such dogma. Throughout his career he showed a remarkable ability to foresee and adapt new trends in modern design. His Depression-era homes are the quintessential examples of what might be termed "Hollywood Moderne," with large windows, dramatic cantilevers, pocket-doors, and luxurious materials like mahogany and chrome. He even included occasional flowerboxes and fountains.

His success, though short lived, can be attributed to a combination of his design talent, his ability to build his homes on a modest budget, and his considerable skills as a salesman and promoter. Just sixteen months after his burst of creativity began, Kesling's Streamline career ended when he pled guilty to fraud

Left to right: The Vanderpool house (1935). Estes House (1935).

and was sentenced, in March 1937, to the California state penitentiary at San Quentin. After futilely battling unhappy clients, extortion, misinformed police detectives, and the courts, he endured criminal conviction, professional ruin, and financial insolvency. Two years after the founding of Kesling Modern Structures, he disappeared from the Los Angeles area and, more disappointingly, from the annals of Los Angeles modern designers.

Three years later, Kesling returned to modern design and construction in San Diego County, where he enjoyed even greater success. During the Second World War he designed and built admirable pre-fabricated civilian housing for war production workers that were applauded by *California Arts+Architecture*. After the war he built many wonderful, compact homes that efficiently addressed California's acute postwar housing shortage. Kesling also designed and erected custom homes that were featured in many publications, including *LIFE* magazine, *Better Homes and*

Gardens, and *House Beautiful*. In a sad repeat of his prewar experience, this chapter also ended badly with Kesling forced from practice under an ethical cloud. Once again his reputation precluded his designs' receipt of the recognition they were due.

The life and career of William Kesling offers a useful means with which to view twentieth century Southern California. His determination and optimism, his practices, and his financial booms and busts all mirror events and conditions of the era. Whatever the circumstances of his successes, it is Kesling's "scintillating structures," not his methods, that are remembered. Kesling's projects exist today because of his unrealistic expectations, unbending drive, and overstated representations—all characteristics that contributed to his ultimate failure. Yet now, nearly seventy years later, his troubles are largely forgotten and his marvelous Streamline homes remain lasting monuments to his unquestionable talent.

kesling
modern
structures

CHAPTER

EARLY YEARS

Anyone familiar with Adolph and Pauline Kessling would not be surprised by the course of their son William's life. Both parents set strong examples of independence and determination. Both displayed entrepreneurial skill and daring. They suffered repeated financial and personal misfortunes but persevered each time. William shared these same characteristics and, throughout his life, they served to both his benefit and detriment.

Like William, German-born Adolph Kessling was a tall, handsome, imposing man. He loved the space and solitude of the outdoors. He was known for his kindly manner, impulsiveness, and speculative business ventures. At just thirteen, he ran away from home and traveled to Russia, where he was taken in by a butcher and his wife. He came alone to America as a young man. Lured to Kansas City by the booming cattle trade, he met and married another German immigrant, Pauline Heissler. For the next forty years, she shared in Adolph's many financial successes and failures and endured his personal failings. William's mother, the petite Pauline Heissler Kessling, had enormous strength and persistence. She was described as being "as sweet a person you would want to meet." Her marriage to Adolph began well and, within twelve years, they acquired a cattle ranch, slaughterhouse, and butcher shop in Brenham, Texas. They raised five children, William being the fourth. During the first 25 years of marriage, Pauline tended to the five children and operated the ranch while Adolph ran their business ventures. Despite certain financial successes, personal difficulties led Adolph to abandon Pauline and four of his children. In 1911, Adolph, with his eldest son, left the family without word as to their whereabouts or intentions. In typical Kessling fashion, Pauline's response was to work still harder, managing both the ranch and their businesses with great success. Five years after disappearing, Adolph wrote Pauline from Calexico, where he had established a new home and successful cattle enterprise, seeking reconciliation. She and the children rejoined him but, displaying more independence, she purchased a separate home nearby and they never again lived as husband and wife.

In the mid-1920s, lured by yet another speculative opportunity, Adolph sold his Calexico business to prospect for gold in the desolate Anza-Borrego portion of the Mojave Desert. At this time, Pauline moved to La Jolla with William's eldest brother where he resumed the family's retail marketing tradition. For the next two years the family members took turns supplying provisions to Adolph's lonely camp in the low desert. It seemed, in retirement, the Kesslings finally enjoyed what each had been seeking. Pauline lived comfortably in her bungalow in La Jolla and Adolph enjoyed his adventure and solitude in the desert.

Left: Just as Kesling's office in Silverlake promoted his streamline designs, his La Jolla office (c. 1950) showed the potential of his postwar design.

Kesling Family Archive

In 1928, Adolph, aged 74, was tragically killed while prospecting. It was surmised that he accidentally pitched himself over a precipice while wielding a pick. After a lifetime of risk-taking, the odds finally turned fatally against him. All these parental examples of bold risk-taking, endurance, and determination helped mold William Kesling in ways that repeated throughout his life. There can be little doubt that Kesling's own tenacious pursuit of daring business ventures and his self-confident spirit were shaped by his parents' example.

After William arrived in Calexico at the age of sixteen, he began to work for his father at various odd jobs, but quickly gravitated toward the construction trade. In this period of America's rapid growth, he easily found work around Calexico and, among other ventures, took a job managing construction on a 12,000–acre ranch just over the Mexican border. His ability to draw and imagine had an obvious parallel in construction carpentry, and the potential of a career became apparent to Kesling. It was only a matter of time before Kesling's inherited ambition would combine with his love of the building trade to bring him to the center of the post-World War I western expansion, Los Angeles.

With its fast-growing population and commensurate building boom, Los Angeles was the ideal place to make a career. He quickly found work as a carpenter's apprentice and settled into a studio apartment in central Los Angeles. Carpentry suited him well as the medium allowed him to combine his skill with an understanding of massing and spatial relationships. It also taught Kesling the importance of materials and the building process in terms of economical design. During this time Kesling

Left: William Kesling, La Jolla (c. 1950).

began to refine his personal style too. He grew a thin mustache and began to comb his hair straight back, giving him a Ronald Coleman-like look. He even redesigned his name by dropping one 's'. He told his disapproving parents the new spelling "just looks better," while he responded to others' questions by asking, "Why do you need two esses?"

Kesling proved an able and ambitious employee who quickly mastered his trade and prided himself on his no-nonsense approach and personal rapport with his fellow workers. Thanks to the boom's expanding demand for skilled construction workers, he soon was promoted to carpenter, then carpentry foreman. Within three years he had risen to the position of superintendent for the Jarboe Construction Co., where he learned general project management and other skills necessary to attain his goal of becoming a general contractor. Within another year, Kesling said he felt equipped to strike out alone into the contracting business, "first contracting carpenter labor, then slowly branching out into the field of general contracting." Operating as a general contractor allowed him to merge his construction skills into his real love, the practice of building design. Initially Kesling designed and built many of the styles popular in late 1920s Los Angeles, from Spanish Revival to Tudor. Even with these otherwise ordinary architectural styles, Kesling's unique talent with spatial arrangement, window placement, and detailing is evident.

Concurrent with this time of rapid professional advancement, Kesling met the twenty-one year old Ehrma Williams, a recent arrival from southern Arizona who was training to be a nurse. The much taller William literally swept the petite Ehrma off her feet. They loved to dance and Ehrma often appeared to glide along as if held above the dance floor by his arms. They fell deeply in love and, after a short courtship, began a fifty-seven year marriage. They settled into a modest apartment in a four-plex owned by Ehrma's mother. Like Kesling's mother, Ehrma was soft-spoken, belying her competence and industriousness. Trained as a nurse, Ehrma was a caregiver all her life. Once married, this vocation was largely directed towards her husband. She became invaluable to Kesling's business success, acting as his infallible memory for all the business and social details he often forgot. When he entered the contracting business she kept the books and handled other office functions. "He was the creativity and she handled the business end," Kesling's niece observed.

Kesling's contracting business was not immune from the sharp cycles of expansion and contraction that characterized Los Angeles' growth and, in 1927, he suspended operations temporarily. During this time Kesling returned to work at Jarboe Construction. He also claimed to have worked as a part-time draftsman for Rudolph Schindler, but no positive evidence of this relationship exists. When building conditions again improved Kesling resumed his contracting business. After the great collapse of 1929, Ehrma, who had begun to work in Kesling's office, returned to work as a nurse to supplement their income. This boom-bust cycle would continue to characterize Kesling's career. Whether or not Kesling ever actually worked for Schindler, he certainly understood the potential of the modernistic style. He sensed the possibilities of offering modern design to budget-minded, middle-class homebuyers. From this concept Kesling Modern Structures was born.

CHAPTER

LOS ANGELES

In 1929 Dr. Philip Lovell, health and fitness columnist for the *Los Angeles Times*, opened his just-completed, Neutra-designed house of the future to public review. Over 15,000 Angelinos came to see this dramatic example of modern design. Though it was publicized as an example of the healthful living then available to those with modern taste and sensibilities, few took note that the home cost over $50,000 to construct and therefore was well beyond the means of the vast majority of Americans. Providing efficient and affordable housing to a growing world was a major tenet of modern design, yet very little had been built that actually met these ideals. The collapse of the construction industry and the subsequent housing crisis in the Great Depression made this failure even more obvious. Kesling recognized this failure and saw the opportunity it offered.

A major obstacle which Kesling believed he could overcome was public taste. Americans marveled at modernistic movie houses, retail stores, even service stations; they were proud to use civic facilities of that style. But to expect them to actually spend their days and nights living in a Streamline home seemed unrealistic. Most Americans probably would have agreed with H. L. Mencken's sentiment, deriding the International Style modern homes of the designer Le Corbusier as "florid chicken coops …

(with) ghastly imitations of the electric chair that the Modernists make of gas-pipe." Kesling was confident his stylish design, salesmanship, and affordable prices would combine to overcome this attitude. Finding a client in the Depression era with both the daring and money to erect a modernistic home was extremely difficult. Yet Los Angeles was probably the only setting where such clients could be found in sufficient numbers. The film colony, in particular, offered a potential clientele for Kesling. Despite reasons for caution, he decided it was time to test the acceptance of his modern home design. Kesling had always prided himself as a hands-on, self-trained, commonsense contractor who knew more about designing and building with economy of materials and labor than many of his college-trained peers. He believed he possessed a rare combination of design talent and practical construction know-how that would allow him to erect what others had not: affordable modernistic housing.

In early 1934 Kesling decided to risk building a model home on speculation. He purchased a small, steep hillside lot in the then-sparsely populated Silverlake district for just $250. Pooling his meager savings with money borrowed from his frugal mother-in-law, he raised the funds to build his first modernistic house. He was confident that this house would demonstrate his

Left: Kesling had a large presence in the newly formed Silverlake tract. Inset: In both wording and style, Kesling's signage had much in common with many of Los Angeles' most polished land promoters.

The Beery house's (1936) unique, winged gateways are reminiscent of the Pan Pacific Auditorium.

talent and clients would soon take notice. On August 1, 1934, with his plans complete, a construction permit was issued. The budget was just $3,600, or $2.55 per square foot (Kesling claimed $2.25), compared to over $10 per square foot to construct the previously mentioned Lovell house. As this was the first time that many of his tradesmen had dealt with certain new materials and methods, construction took 10 months. The fact that it took almost one year with his full supervision should have been a reason for concern. Kesling's home succeeded beyond his most optimistic expectations. He later recalled with pride, "This house attracted so much attention that without much effort I signed contracts to erect 35 houses of similar design." In addition, he

negotiated a deal with Deardon's department store whereby they furnished his model home in return for the use of the pictures of the interior in their catalogs and advertising materials.

In the latter half of 1935 he filed permits to build four homes each budgeted at $4,000. In addition he broke ground on his own office on Silverlake Boulevard near Effie Street. He would eventually erect a dozen buildings within walking distance of this office. He broke ground on another eleven homes in the first half of 1936. Seemingly out of nowhere, Kesling emerged to challenge, and in some respects surpass, his more-famous, well-trained peers. At a time when many eminent architects had no work or struggled with just a few commissions (Rudolph Schindler

Concurrently with his home project, Kesling built this duplex in West Hollywood for Wallace Beery. (1936)

began just four projects during all of 1935), Kesling Modern Structures thrived. After 14 years of diligent self-preparation and unwavering confidence combined with uncommon talent, Kesling had rightfully taken his place in Streamline Moderne Los Angeles. As one might expect, the Hollywood film community provided the core of Kesling's clients. They had the bold taste, social outlook, and confidence to build such homes. Just as important, they had the income.

Kesling Modern Structures' most famous client was the actor Wallace Beery, who was so enamored with Kesling's designs that he signed a contract for two projects simultaneously. On June 13, 1936, Kesling received a permit to build a duplex for Beery on Harper Avenue in West Hollywood. Two days later, he received a permit to build a second Los Angeles home for Beery near the Goldwyn Studios where he was under contract. It was clearly one of Kesling's most important houses. From the whimsical front gate and dramatic rear windows to its open floor plan and rooftop sundeck, it was perhaps his most unrestrained home. It epitomized Kesling's talent for transforming the austere International style with windows, curves, light, and drama into a uniquely Southern California expression.

Kesling's enormous success raises some important questions. First, how did he attract so many clients? In the depth of the Depression, total annual housing starts in the city of Los Angeles numbered in just the hundreds. Kesling's model home was built on a lightly traveled, undeveloped, dead-end street in the Silverlake district. Surely he could not have relied on off-the-street sales. Just what did Kesling mean when he remarked that he signed 35 contracts without much effort, as such success seems impossible without "much effort"? The style and verbiage of his signs suggest that great effort and consideration were put into promotion of his image. How important were his prices as a lure to potential clients? Kesling's homes were priced at or below conventional, comparably sized and appointed homes and well below the cost one would expect for such a modern, custom design. He confidently stated, "The contracts were signed from $2.60 to $3.00 per square foot. This showed a nice margin of profit over the cost of the original structure." If it cost $2.55 per square foot to build the model home, then these prices imply a profit between 2–17%, leaving no margin for error on Kesling's part. Perhaps Kesling was too sharp with his pencil. Perhaps he was too driven to achieve his goal of providing reasonably priced, modern homes. Most likely, Kesling's optimism made him unrealistic about his ability to deliver on his plans and promises. Additionally, how did Kesling intend to manage all these projects? If it took 10 months of full-time, hands-on supervision to build one house, how long would it take, with little of Kesling's personal supervision, to build 35 houses? His ambitious commitments required him to act as designer, builder, and financial agent and allowed him to boast that "We made the plans and specifications, secured the financing, and erected these structures." By taking on every task, he was maximizing both the risk to himself

and his responsibility to the client. If any aspect of a project were to go wrong, Kesling could look only to himself for remedy. Others would look only to him for blame.

Carried on a wave of unsuspecting clients, Kesling Modern Structures moved ambitiously ahead, simultaneously erecting homes in Silverlake, West Hollywood, Sunset Plaza, the San Fernando Valley, Pasadena, and Westwood. There is no evidence that Kesling understood the seriousness of his situation. Material and labor prices began recovering from the extremely depressed levels of 1934, cutting into Kesling's slim profit margin. Although relevant government statistics were not kept in 1935, it is estimated that construction labor costs in Southern California rebounded as much 16% within the year after Kesling completed his model home. This alone could have been enough to sink Kesling's booming business. "With prices continually rising, the profit was fast being eaten up," he conceded later. Finding competent tradesmen and supervisors proved to be an even bigger problem. With so many projects, Kesling was lucky to average half a day per week at each job site. Without his regular supervision or that of a competent supervisor, the projects could not proceed efficiently. Kesling lamented,

"The general construction of these houses was completely different and new to the mechanics and subcontractors. The fact that I had 35 contracts meant that I could not supervise them personally. Therefore I tried to secure a superintendent with knowledge of this particular type of construction. I soon found this was impossible, as people with a thorough knowl-

Right: The Vanderpool house (1936) second of the twins, built in Silverlake, nearing completion.

for information regarding
these modern scintillating structures

INQUIRE

KESLING ★

MODERN STRUCTURES

Complete BUILDING & FINANCING

1639 SILVER LAKE BLVD.   Phone OL 6038

edge of this particular type of construction were limited to a few architects, a few students, a few college professors, and myself. I tried numerous superintendents and found it necessary to continually change workmen. With the large number of houses going, it was impossible for me to supervise personally ..."

By April of 1936, with his projects grinding to a standstill and prices rising rapidly, Kesling could no longer ignore his situation. As might his parents, Kesling and his wife responded with still greater determination and effort. "Even with this situation," Kesling noted, "my wife and I, by working from ten to fifteen hours per day, seven days a week, were slowly but surely mastering this situation." Kesling never considered curtailing his business activities, not even long enough to regain his financial footing. In fact, the number of his jobs in progress peaked in June of 1936, three months after Kesling first realized his precarious financial position. During this month, he started an astounding five new projects. Perhaps he hoped to make enough profit on this new work to cover his losses on the original projects. Between his lack of funds and lack of qualified workmen, progress on his projects became impossible. In desperation, Kesling enlisted the services of the Construction Loan Services Company as his agent to take over Kesling Modern Structures' unfinished projects. Although this amounted to putting his business in a kind of receivership, Kesling seemed relieved with this arrangement as the projects slowly progressed toward completion. Unburdened of the responsibilities now assigned to Construction Loan Services, Kesling began signing new contracts for design and supervision

services only, for a straight percentage. Additionally, he agreed to deposit this new revenue into a fund to cover any deficits on the outstanding projects being completed by Construction Loan Services. After explaining this arrangement to his clients, Kesling commented that "most of the owners cooperated 100%, realizing what we were up against, but we had a few of them that were impossible to deal with, and made the job doubly hard."

During this time of financial difficulty, Kesling made some ill-advised arrangements. In early 1936, representing himself as a Mr. Francis F. Williams, he opened a checking account at the First National Bank of Glendale. In what was clearly an attempt to shield himself from the coming financial crisis, funds from Kesling's projects began to find their way into this account. When this activity was uncovered later, Kesling vehemently denied any wrongdoing. "My contracts with the owners were all written assigning all the funds to me ... for the purpose of erecting the building," he maintained. "There were no strings attached, as to the method they were to be paid out. These funds were to be paid ... to whom I designated, on my order." Kesling stubbornly resented any questioning of his practices.

These infractions may have gone undetected had it not been for William Greene, the one client who refused to assign his contract to Construction Loan Services upon Kesling's request. In the spring of 1936, Kesling Modern Structures began erecting a project for Mr. and Mrs. Greene on their lot on Riverside Drive in North Hollywood. Having already built a cottage at the rear of this lot, the Greenes now wanted Kesling to build a larger house at the front. No one could have guessed how bad this business relationship would sour. Within weeks of the groundbreaking, Greene became convinced of Kesling's dishonesty and made himself an unrelenting enemy. Kesling stated that, "... they [the Greenes] were, without a doubt, the most unreasonable people I have ever erected a building for." Kesling accused Greene of leading a group that "went from [his] job to the jobs of others, continually causing trouble. Seemingly not competent to see the situation as it really was, they imagined and floated all kinds of preposterous stories." On June 1, 1936, Mr. Greene came storming into the new offices Kesling Modern Structures had built on Silverlake Boulevard, demanding that Kesling immediately accompany him to the Hayward Lumber Company (the disbursement trustee for his project). He said he had discovered evidence of Kesling's embezzlement. Once there, Kesling tried to explain that the checks represented perfectly legitimate reimbursements for goods and services for which Kesling Modern Structures had forwarded payment. Mr. Greene could not be convinced and was only satisfied when Kesling redeposited a check for the full $350 in question. Over the summer, after visiting several other Kesling houses, Mr. Greene chose steel sash windows

Contractor, Wife Indict

22 Builders Swindled, Police Charge

William P. Kesling, building contractor, and his wife, Ehrma, were indicted by the County Grand Jury yesterday on charges of forgery of false labor and material claims as a result of an investigation by the police bunko detail of an asserted building scandal.

Twenty-two home builders in Los Angeles and the San Fernando Valley have been left high and dry, with unfinished homes and their building funds exhausted, by the Keslings' operations, asserted Detective Lieuts. Jerry Moore and Charles Riblett.

Kesling and his wife were jailed yesterday under $1500 bond to await arraignment in Superior Court.

According to Moore, Kesling, who does business as Kesling Modern Structures, arranged loans for prospective home builders and named trustees to handle the building funds. As the buildings progressed, he issued false labor and material claims against the trustees, received checks to cover the claims, and together with his wife, who is his bookkeeper, forged indorsements of the checks and cashed them, according to the indictment.

Fire Kills Six of Family; Two Others May Die

Accused

WILLIAM P. KESLING (above), contractor, was indicted yesterday for allegedly presenting false claims for work done. Kesling, according to police, exhausted the funds of 22 home builders.—Daily News Photo.

25

of Kesling's design, which he saw in Kesling's Johnstone house in Los Feliz. Knowing how difficult this client was, Kesling made doubly sure of Greene's selection, even sending a sample over for his approval before ordering their manufacture. In the fall, after the windows were manufactured to custom specifications, delivered, and nearly completely installed, Mr. Greene decided they were not acceptable after all. His business funds already exhausted, Kesling didn't know how to respond to such irrational behavior. It appears that having caught Kesling in somewhat unethical practices, Mr. Greene was going to use this knowledge to his maximum advantage. Kesling found himself facing his toughest obstacle yet—the first obstacle that he might not be able to overcome. According to Kesling, at one point the Greenes and another man named Rose came "wildly" into Kesling's office and asked to see him in private. Mr. Greene then launched into the following "tirade of abuse":

"[Mr. Greene] told me that I had gone about cheating poor, defenseless people long enough and that he was going to put a stop to it and send me away to the penitentiary for 35 years, and my wife for only 25 years as he felt sorry for her, unless we paid him $1,000 right there, and he was going to finish his own house, and if we didn't, he would call the police on the checks mentioned previously. Mrs. Greene stood with her hand on the phone. I was convinced I had done nothing out of the way, so I told Mrs. Greene to call the police."

Kesling believed that Mrs. Greene was a former employee of either the police department or the district attorney's office and he had reason to fear the threat. Still, he stubbornly held his

ground. Having heard the conversation from the outer office, Ehrma entered and begged the Greenes not to cause further trouble. She told them that they did not have $1,000, but were willing to let the Greenes hold the deed to their office on Silverlake Boulevard as a bond to prove that they would complete the house. The Keslings additionally agreed to pay for the manufacture of different casement windows by a different steel sash company of Mr. Greene's choosing. Having submitted under duress to these concessions, the Keslings hoped for at least a short respite from the Greenes' relentless threats. Again, they underestimated the Greenes' capacity to cause trouble. In early November, the Greenes began calling on other clients of Kesling Modern Structures, trying to enlist their support to file a formal complaint against William and Ehrma. Several clients called Kesling to warn him about these visits and how the Greenes solicited each client "to join in with them, and go to the district attorney's office and assist them, as they needed as many as they could get to interest [him]" in filing charges. Four different clients independently related a similar story, though none of them agreed to join the Greene's "scheme". One client described how she "... almost bodily ejected Mrs. Greene from her place." Despite these testimonials from Kesling's supporters, it cannot be overlooked that three clients did agree to support the Greenes' complaint.

On November 13, Los Angeles Police Department detective lieutenants Gerald Moore and Charles Riblett called at Kesling's office and asked William and Ehrma to accompany them downtown for questioning. Kesling would later recount that, upon arrival downtown, "We were immediately booked [on the charge of forgery] and I was taken to the city jail and my wife to Lincoln Heights jail." Unable to post bail, they both remained incarcerated for the next six days. After hearing the testimony of the Greenes and the other witnesses at the preliminary hearing, the judge summarily dismissed the case, freeing the Keslings. According to Kesling, at the conclusion of the proceedings a visibly upset Detective Moore told Kesling's attorney that he would immediately "get out another complaint." At the time, Kesling commented that "You will find...evidently the one object on the arresting officer's mind was to get a conviction, regardless how. He certainly did not try to get the facts."

Grand jury proceedings against the Keslings began almost immediately. The list of those questioned under oath included Detective Moore, Mr. Greene, three other clients, the employees and suppliers to whom the checks were made, the bank cashier, an officer of the lumberyard, and the Keslings themselves. A bitter Kesling stated, "The grand jury was a farce. The evidence was presented to them in a manner in which it was impossible for them to do otherwise but to vote an indictment." On December 8, 1936, just fifteen days after having the charges initially dismissed, William and Ehrma were indicted on a total of 15 counts of "forgery of endorsement." After another two nights in jail, they posted a combined bail of $2,000 and were released to prepare for trial.

Several important aspects of the indictments cannot be denied. They allege repeated fraud and forgery, perpetrated with near-equal responsibility by William and Ehrma. In some ways the indictments involving Ehrma may be perceived as even more serious, as she was accused of physically forging the checks. One indictment alleges the creation of a fictitious employee, one M. Becnal, for whom checks were drawn and cashed by the Keslings. Another claims the Keslings had checks made out to an account for one Ilot Johnson, who was in fact employed as a sleeping-car conductor and did not even know the Keslings. William felt that the indictments against Ehrma were particularly unfair and that Deputy District Attorney Galliano was using them as a lever against him. Nowhere in Kesling's lengthy explanation of the intricacies of his financial arrangements, and the mitigating factors surrounding these charges, does he explain why M. Becnal and Ilot Johnson appear on his payrolls. Neither does he explain why he used the alias Francis F. Williams.

Conversely, the indictments were of little financial value. The total fraud claimed in all fifteen counts against the Keslings was $315. The seven counts relating to the Greenes' home amounted to just $128.30. The three other projects that were the subjects of the remaining counts alleged losses of between $77.50 and $7.50 each. Some of the counts amounted to exceedingly small sums of money; the first count against Ehrma charged her with forging the endorsement on a $4.80 check. In addition, all four projects connected to the indictments had been satisfactorily completed before the trial. According to Kesling, all jobs were "complete" and "all bills paid," except for the Greene project, for which Kesling was still owed $1,600. An investigator reported that "... those persons for whom he built homes apparently got what they paid for and in some instances a great deal more." He added, however, that the Greenes felt they were owed $1,900 from Kesling, rather than owing him $1,600.

Getting a grand jury indictment for such a small amount raises additional questions. How much was this case driven by Greene's alleged contacts with law enforcement? How much was driven by a popular skepticism toward modern design in general? Was this all the evidence that could be proven against Kesling, or were these just the most ironclad examples of a multitude of wrongdoings? To what extent did the desperate, suspicious atmosphere of Depression society dispose people to react strongly against financial misdeeds and readily believe the worst about others, particularly those espousing new ideas? None of these questions can be definitively answered.

Regardless of the facts or outcome of the trial, Kesling Modern Structures was ruined. An afternoon tabloid featured the story with a headline proclaiming Kesling had "swindled 22 builders," accompanied by his jailhouse mug shot. The text sensationally charged that the victimized homebuilders "were left high and dry with unfinished homes and their building funds exhausted, by the Kesling operations ..." In an era so recently traumatized by the panic of collapse, repairing the damage of such press—whether it was true or not—was nearly impossible. Kesling observed, "The owners that were influenced by the Greenes... became panicky and took [the jobs] out of [our] hands. They [the projects] are now standing incomplete and going to ruin. The percentage contracts that were signed were returned and the contracts cancelled." Professionally and financially ruined, his wife facing prison, Kesling uncharacteristically capitulated without a fight. "My business has been destroyed," he lamented. "I am penniless, my wife's health is broken, and we have borrowed everything my wife's parents had." Rather than defend an already lost cause and risk his wife's conviction, on January 28, 1937, in front of judge Dudley Valentine,

Kesling pled guilty to one count involving $24, with the understanding that all the charges against Ehrma would be dropped. A trial would have gone a long way toward clarifying the degree of Kesling's guilt and perhaps the motives of the people against him. With his guilty plea, no evidence was actually tested in court. Without a trial and its transcript, the closest thing to an unbiased record of the issues surrounding the case comes from the ancillary arrest and probation reports. In his report to the judge, deputy probation officer George Grist stated,

"The defendant's trouble appears to be that of one who has bitten off more than he could chew and as a result became so involved that he reverted to somewhat illegal tactics in order to keep his head above water. The defendant also apparently used some shady means in trying to get his client to pay additional for extras in order to make up for some shortage in another place. This however appears to be the method in meeting competition in many lines of business ... probation officer cannot find where the defendant has profited by any of his activities."

Describing his visits with the project owners involved in the case, Grist stated that besides Greene, all three were satisfied and/or pleased with their homes. These three were the same individuals who testified against Kesling to the grand jury. As for the Greenes, the same probation officer noted that they "are living in a small modern house which the defendant built on the rear of their lot, and on the front of the lot is a completed house built by the defendant." Even more appalling is that they kept the deed to the office that the Keslings had put up as a bond and sold it in November of 1937. After doing everything Greene could to impede Kesling's progress by inciting others, contributing to his insolvency, extorting him with threats, and then filing a formal complaint with the district attorney, Greene completed his vengeful streak of actions by selling Kesling's office and keeping the proceeds.

On March 4, 1937, William Kesling stood for sentencing before Judge Valentine, who pronounced, "It is the judgment and sentence of this court that you be sentenced to the San Quentin Penitentiary for the term prescribed by law; however, sentence will be suspended and you will be placed on probation for a period of two years ... the defendant [will] refrain from carrying on any contracting business during this period of probation." With that statement, Kesling Modern Structures officially ceased business. A rapid two-year ascent led to complete decline. To survive, the ruined Kesling took a job selling steel sash. Interestingly, there are four houses on which ground was broken after Kesling's arrest, two of these started after Kesling pled guilty. In accordance with the requirements of Kesling's probation, others contracted the construction of these houses. Yet the houses clearly had the trademark Kesling design and features, suggesting that they had begun the design phase before his arrest.

The real tragedy of this episode was not Kesling's but that of Los Angeles itself. Kesling's buildings became nonentities in the annals of Los Angeles modern design. Kesling's scandal allowed the architectural establishment to look down at this uneducated interloper and hold him up as an example of the dangers of not hiring professional architects with proper credentials. Despite leaving his wide and distinctive mark on the modern design landscape of Los Angeles, it was as if William Kesling never existed. Worse still for his legacy, his homes were shunned and neglected. Having high maintenance requirements, particularly the floors, roofs, and windows, most developed leaks and suffered extensive, chronic water damage. Kesling's tarnished reputation and the postwar distaste for streamline modern style led to disuse and indiscriminant renovation of his houses. By the 1970s seven projects had been razed, most after falling into extreme disrepair. A further nine have been remodeled beyond recognition or restoration. One of these is now covered with redwood shingles, another now has a Moorish theme, complete with minarets, and still another is now vaguely reminiscent of Cape Cod. Another home was either wrongly completed by the contractor who took over for Kesling, or was badly altered thereafter. Almost all have had ill-advised additions or updating. Of the 35 that were built, 20 have survived somewhat intact. Only a handful of these retain their original layout and fixtures.

CHAPTER  3

ʃAN DIEGO

Penniless and depressed, with both his reputation and the courts precluding further practice of his trade, it seemed that at age 38 Kesling's career was finished. With the trial no longer restricting him, he quit his job selling steel window sash and left town, never again to reside in Los Angeles. Looking back on that period, Kesling noted that, in total, he had "erected over 450 homes, stores, and apartments, etc., in Los Angeles and its vicinity." Despite this incredible contribution, he quickly became a forgotten man. Kesling wrote that he spent the years between 1937 and 1939 in Salinas, California, and then San Francisco, where he "designed and built contemporary homes, stores, and apartments." Under the terms of his probation, any such work could only be done as an employee of another contractor, so no record of his work at this time exists.

His probation ended in 1939 and Kesling decided to resume his career in La Jolla, where his family had settled a dozen years earlier. Whether he fully realized the opportunities presented by this sleepy seaside community is not known. With his optimism restored, he entered this venture with his characteristic confidence and ambition. Kesling re-formed Kesling Modern Structures and built a modern office in the center of La Jolla. Employing his ample knowledge and experience to this new enterprise, Kesling quickly established himself in the building community of La Jolla. Having been given the time-honored, California "second chance," he redeemed himself by succeeding. One of his first major commissions, the Kaysor house, shows just how much his

style evolved in his two and a half-year hiatus. Though he built Spanish Revival and English Tudor homes in the 1920s and Streamline in the 1930s, his designs now changed to a postwar look. Wood replaced much of the stucco and all of the steel. Once again he parlayed his talent, design, salesmanship, and his taste for speculation into a successful enterprise.

The Second World War captured Kesling's attention and fundamentally altered the course of his career. The military's increased presence in San Diego, requiring housing for both defense-industry workers and military personnel, made the provision of this needed housing a major priority. Architects and builders throughout the country studied solutions to the critical housing shortage. In 1942, Kesling was awarded a contract to design and build one hundred, 750-square-foot, prefabricated,

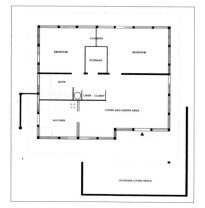

demountable, single-family dwellings at 46th and Market streets in San Diego, for newly arriving aircraft-industry workers. Kesling was proud of the construction method, noting, "These were erected in less time and at a lower cost than any other prefabs constructed during the war in San Diego County." The November,

Left: The Kaysor house (1942) in La Jolla was one of Kesling's first projects after reestablishing himself.

31

Above: In his wartime housing Kesling used 2 x 4 wood framing and either Cemestos or glass, note the thinness of the roof. Left: After the war, despite some disapproval (they were dubbed, "Kesling's Kozy Kowsheds" by the architectural critic for the *Los Angeles Times*), Kesling quickly built and sold a block's worth of his low-cost homes in La Jolla.

1942, issue of *California Arts+Architecture* featured this project, commenting that "in the 100 [houses] designed by Mr. Kesling, the emphasis was on modern architecture, and the result is pleasing ... the architect attained simplification by elimination." Many of these supposedly demountable, prefabricated dwellings still remain. These houses possessed almost no similarities with Kesling's earlier, Streamline work. The windows were wood frame, not steel casement, and often centered rather than placed in a room's corner. With neither parapets nor attics, the light-weight roofs gave the houses an almost gossamer feel. The fences surrounding the patios employed an unusual and original Kesling innovation. Rather than build his fences with standard, upright posts and cross framing to support vertical planks, Kesling used 2 x 10 horizontal planks without cross framing at all, saving both labor and materials. The 4 x 8-foot prefabricated wall panels were anchored to slab floors. These panels consisted of 2 x 4-inch wood frames with three-quarter-inch sheets of Cemestos, a mixture

of cement and asbestos, suspended between. Only in wartime San Diego would two-inch thick roofs and three-quarter inch thick walls in unheated homes be acceptable. This work taught Kesling valuable lessons for the postwar housing market he was entering. The economic and social dislocations caused by the transition to peacetime produced a severe housing crunch. At precisely the time when demand for housing was surging, building materials, of which manufacture had been diverted to war production, were in short supply. Kesling understood that his wartime designs could save materials and bring affordable, new housing to the market. The lessons of thrift and economy that Kesling learned during the Depression also suited this situation.

In 1946, Kesling purchased twelve of what may have been La Jolla's least-expensive lots on which to test his theory. Working from his basic floor plan, Kesling erected several variations as models. His new designs had larger rooms than his war-era houses, as well as heat, sliding doors, and carports. These homes

also had more working windows, though most were still fixed panes of glass with simple wood moldings as stops. The many improvements over his wartime projects, particularly the larger scale, gave the homes a pleasant feel of space and light. In the extreme postwar housing shortage, this project met with immediate success and Kesling soon expanded this model to other La Jolla locations. This project attracted attention from more than just potential homeowners. Architectural publications also reviewed his new projects. In an obvious slap at Kesling's earlier self-characterization of his modern houses as "scintillating structures," the *Los Angeles Times' Home Magazine* referred to the new homes as "Kesling's Kozy Kowsheds." Not all the reviews were so derisive. Architectural critic Ethel McCall Head stated, "One of the more interesting views we have found here [in La Jolla] is Dowling Drive, which I believe is the only place in the United States where an entire block of all-modern prefabricated homes can be found."

More important to Kesling's local reputation were the opinions of La Jolla's leading citizens. They had a clear vision of La Jolla as a re-creation of a seaside Mediterranean village, based on the Spanish Revival look exemplified in Bertram Goodhue's designs for the 1935 Pan-Pacific Exhibition. To them, the inexpensive, modern eyesores erected by nonconformists like Kesling were a scourge on the community. Russell Forrester, who practiced modern architecture in La Jolla after World War II, commented, "In La Jolla, there was a continuous battle with the city because they didn't like flat roofs. You couldn't build a carport. You couldn't call it a carport, so you called it a breezeway or you called it something else. We had all kinds of terms we used in order to get building permits on things that were illegal, or not really illegal, but frowned upon by the city." Kesling had his own peculiar way of dealing with the many obstacles he faced. Forrester stated that he certainly wasn't political, and he didn't

do anything to try to help matters, but, in his own quiet way, just the mere fact that he was building modern homes made a difference. "He was one of the fighters who helped bring it about that we could have contemporary architecture in La Jolla." As he had in the past, Kesling responded to his critics by moving forward with full confidence and determination, but critics, clients, and the law had all made Kesling sensitive to scrutiny and he often responded by employing a strategy of evasion. "He would do buildings without building permits and then if they caught him, he would then just pay whatever it [the fine] was," Forrester claimed. "He always felt that [the fine] was just the plan-check fee. I bet he built half a dozen buildings with no permit at all. He just got away with it. It was a time when everything was booming and if they didn't catch him, they didn't catch him." When forced to obtain permits, Kesling would always provide the minimum information required. "He was the kind of man that would draw the plans for a permit. That doesn't necessarily mean that's what was built," Forrester added.

Extending his La Jolla success, Kesling built a development of several dozen homes in the Mira Mesa district of San Diego. Aimed again at the postwar housing crunch, these modest houses are a more suburban version of the Dowling Drive project. Appointed with some slightly more luxurious features (such as an enclosed garage and higher ceilings) the houses appear to share the same materials as those on Dowling Drive. The development is most noteworthy for the names of its three residential streets: Kesling Street, Kesling Place, and Kesling Court.

As the postwar transition proceeded, demand for luxury homes returned and Kesling resumed his favorite endeavors: custom design and construction. Combining some of the basic

Right: In another development northeast of San Diego, Kesling Street intersects Kesling Court.
Left: The small enclosed garden patio in the King house (1947) was another way Kesling brought in the outdoors.

Julius Shulman

elements of his "kowsheds," such as the roofs, the windows, and the sliding doors with brick and space, he created beautiful homes at reasonable costs. Four homes in particular, erected in 1946, illustrate his return to custom modern construction. The Gamson and Ingall houses in La Jolla offer good examples of Kesling's use of his pre-fab knowledge in his custom homes. Both employ the same basic wall and roof system as Dowling Drive, but the scale is larger, fireplaces were added, and built-ins were extensively used. The Gamson house was prominently featured in the November 1947 issue of *Better Homes & Gardens* as "Five Star Home #1711." For $5, the magazine offered plans, detailed drawings, specs, material lists, and owner-contractor agreements, everything one would need to construct such a home, available by mail or at Barker Brothers and similar stores across the country. Their building editor, John Normile, AIA, commented, "It is a small house, only 1,196 square feet, hardly larger than the conventional G.I. job. Yet look at what, in the way of good living, it has." Duplicating his Depression era strategy, Kesling succeeded in bringing the unaffordable within reach. In these cases, he was offering beautiful, eminently livable homes in exclusive La Jolla to those who might not otherwise be financially able to purchase them. However, this strategy and its effect on La Jolla increased Kesling's unpopularity with many of the town's leading citizens.

With the King and the Everett houses, the transition from semi-prefabrication to custom, postwar design was complete. Little resemblance to his Dowling Drive project is apparent. Only on the exterior eaves are his roof systems evident. These homes were larger,

Julius Shulman

Above and left: In 1947 the McConnell house in La Jolla appeared in *LIFE* described as a bachelor's home for entertaining. It solidified Kesling's reputation as a custom designer/builder of merit.

and not rectangular. In the King house, elaborate brickwork surrounded the entire house as either balcony railing or wainscoting. A twelve by eight foot, glass-enclosed central courtyard brought sunlight to the center of this more formal house. The ample built-ins were simple and understated. The dining room furniture was also designed by Kesling. The Everett house was also oriented towards the outdoors. It was built with at least one wall of glass in every room. A large outdoor patio and a separate deck faced canyon and ocean views. The living room featured picture windows framing the same views. With hardwood floors, drapes, and traditional furniture, it seems the least modern of Kesling's postwar projects. But when these distractions are peeled away, a clean, modern design remains.

Between 1946 and 1950 Russell Forrester freelanced for Kesling, making working drawings from Kesling's sketches. He later recounted, "I don't think there was a lot of stock building materials at the end of World War II and [Kesling] would think nothing of using something that he could get. If he could get windows, he would use windows, but by and large, fixed windows were always a piece of glass with wood stops and he would have little windows at the top, or bottom, that opened and that was it. The big windows almost never moved so they were always with wood stops and ultimately cheap to do and I remember the building materials being just what ever he could get away with. The lumber was just what he could get a hold of ... They were all [built on] slab ... Very little went into the slabs, including steel!" According to Forrester, Kesling figured that by running heavier decking he could eliminate joists and this labor saving would more than compensate for the higher material costs. Forrester went on to say that, unfortunately, Kesling's tendency toward such thrift sometimes led him to try a span too great a distance, which led to sagging. "You know, if a four-by-four would do it, but a four-by-six looked better, he would use the four-by-four. There

wasn't any question about what he would do. He would use the cheaper approach," Forrester added. It was as if Kesling was following an aesthetic based completely on economy.

In 1946, retired naval officer Walton McConnell commissioned Kesling to design and build a "bachelor's retreat" on a bluff sitting over a La Jolla beach. In this house Kesling left nearly everything from his past behind. Gone are the curves, the stucco, the casement windows and a front door, replaced by triangles and rectangles, wood paneling, and large wood-frame windows. Still, Kesling's sense of drama and light remain and here he returns to a dramatic site like the ones he favored in Silverlake. Without the constraint of a tight budget, Kesling added both height (15 feet in the living room) and space to this house. The spacious living room, almost completely encased in glass, gives the occupants a feeling of being on the beach. The extra volume also allowed for a loft-style bedroom overlooking the living room and offered sweeping views of the shore. All interior paneling was of Costa Rican mahogany. Extensive use of brick in the pathways, patios, and walls, and particularly in the grand living room fireplace, gives the house a sense of weight and security against the crashing waves below. Except for the interruption of this fireplace, guests were almost entirely surrounded by windows, affording a view both up and down the shoreline. In November 1947, *LIFE* magazine visited this bachelor while he entertained and enjoyed the "Riviera-like fun" for which this home was built. In an article entitled "Life Visits a Cliffside House," the editors approvingly commented, "As a setting for this life he [Mr. McConnell] has built himself a dramatic, glassy $40,000 home which hugs the edge of a 50-foot seaside cliff. Here the Pacific swishes around under the living room floor and occasionally splashes up soothingly over the huge windows."

Building both luxury and economy homes of style, Kesling Modern Structures grew well beyond even its prewar success. To

Right: Jamar dining room, location unknown.

Above and right: Front elevation of custom home in La Jolla, Kesling first designed such a rooftop sundeck for the Beery House in 1935, but he did not promote it this well. Note undeveloped La Jolla behind.

Robert Cleveland

satisfy his growing demand for materials, Kesling opened a lumber company next door to his offices. With classic Kesling initiative, he purchased and regularly sent his two trucks up to Oregon to buy cheap lumber. "The rumor was that he was buying lumber in Oregon because no one in California would sell it to him," Forrester joked. These trucks also delivered to his La Jolla projects great quantities of a dubious building material, Cemestos. Years later, in 1964, Kesling wrote that in his career he had "constructed over 3,000 contemporary structures" in the San Diego area. In addition to his thriving business in custom modern

design and construction, Kesling began speculating in land.

After 25 years of hard work, the Keslings finally started to enjoy the fruits of William's success. His niece recalled, "I always got a big bang out of seeing Ehrma and Bill drive up, because he was invariably in something with the top down and he had his tam on; either the plaid cap or the tam." He regularly customized his many cars, once extending a small European convertible by eight inches to accommodate his size. Kesling loved to fish and over the years he owned seven boats. He built one of his first boats himself, at his lumberyard. His last boat

was the Viajero II, a 110-foot, converted sub-chaser he personally customized for fishing and pleasure. Exercising his own carpentry skills, he redesigned and installed the entire wood interior. He regularly hosted parties and excursions on this yacht. His niece remembers being hosted in a "great big beautiful dining room with windows all around." To add comfort to his many hunting trips, primarily in Baja, California, Kesling purchased a four-wheel-drive, army surplus transport and converted it into a custom motor home, which he dubbed "the Rambler." He also returned to Borrego Springs, where his father died, to hunt and then to erect the Borrego Desert Club. This beautiful 5,000-square-foot facility offered an elaborate dining room and a unique, enormous swimming pool set against a view of the mountains surrounding Anza-Borrego. The dining room was sided by nine ten-by-ten-foot glass panes looking out to the desert. The pool was a twelve-foot-deep, thirty-by-sixty-foot ellipse looking out over a pristine desert canyon. Though the club failed after just a few years, it remains nearly intact.

To satisfy their ongoing craving for speculation, William and Ehrma visited both Del Mar and Agua Caliente during their respective seasons. Ehrma took a very businesslike approach and tempered Bill's speculations. They read the *Daily Forum*. A friend of the Keslings stated, "They played the horses everyday. I think they had the racing sheets, played it on the kitchen table." Ehrma insisted that this activity be kept out of the open so as not to risk their reputation. About this time, Kesling told a nephew who had just lost his business, "You're not a success unless you fail sometime. It all goes together. Don't lose heart, just keep trying." Kesling seemed to be living proof.

Those who knew or worked with the Keslings in La Jolla all agree that Ehrma was an integral part of the business. William's niece Gloria remembers her as "the busiest thing in the world ... All her life she took care of people." Russell Forrester stated, "There wasn't any question in my mind. When I wanted to get paid, I talked to Ehrma. She kept a very good set of books. " Though she ably handled the books, Ehrma gave William the center stage in management decisions and relations with clients. She was always available with a fact or name, but she let William do all the talking. In contrast to William's silver tongue and flamboyant style of dress, Ehrma was soft-spoken and dressed simply. Forrester retold how he once gave Kesling a bill for some work and Kesling instructed him to come to his office for payment on Saturday. On Friday, Forrester happened to be in La Jolla and decided to save himself a return trip. When he drove up behind Kesling's office, there was Ehrma packing the car. "What's going on?" he asked. "We're going to Oregon for two weeks vacation," she unknowingly replied. With Forrester standing on the running board, and after much discussion and consternation between the Keslings, Ehrma gave Forrester a check for the amount due, and of course, it bounced.

Just as Kesling seemed to have banished the ghosts of his past forever, his success in La Jolla would again prove fleeting. In a repeat of the 1930s, Kesling found himself overextended, and again he resorted to unethical actions to keep his business afloat. Though the record is fragmentary, many clues, both anecdotal and in the public record, point to a combination of events that cumulated in a second, final failure. Kesling's brother, Edwin, quit working as his accountant due to frustration with Kesling's cavalier attitude toward finances. Court records indicate Kesling was a defendant in an inordinate number of civil law suits for someone practicing his profession at that time. Forrester said it bluntly, "People were buying because of the design. They were suing because of the construction." Many of these civil suits were the result of unpaid loans and other evidence of general financial difficulty and/or malfeasance. It appears that in the late 1950s a Kesling employee, Raymond Goudreau, was partially blinded when a chip from his hammer broke off and

Right: Kesling at the right-hand wheel of his customized sports car. He had a penchant for clothes and cars.

Above: Kesling purchased this van as army surplus and outfitted it for hunting trips to Baja California. Right: Kesling fishing on his own 110-foot yacht, which he used for both entertaining and sport.

struck him. His injury claim exposed the fact that Kesling had been underpaying his workers' compensation contributions over many years. As a result, in 1960 Kesling was sued by the carpenter's union for not contributing to the insurance pool as required.

By 1962, William Kesling had constructed his last structure. Gone were the yacht, the cars and "the Rambler," his property, the lumberyard, and Kesling Modern Structures—everything but his home. At the age of 63, Kesling again found himself wiped out and without a profession. He and Ehrma retreated to their house and thereafter he found sporadic work as a handyman and carpenter in La Jolla. With scrap materials from this work and other modest purchases, he constructed (without a permit) a small apartment on their roof to increase their meager income. William remained vigorous for another ten years, until his mid-seventies, when he developed Alzheimer's disease and diabetes. He died of natural causes on October 13, 1983, at the age of 84. Ehrma was active and alert until her death at age 90, in 1993.

Beyond the personal tragedy of Kesling's second financial failure was the derision and neglect his buildings would once again suffer, as if in punishment for his misdeeds. The propensity for inhabitants of California's beach communities to build and rebuild ever-larger homes resulted in many of Kesling's homes being razed or remodeled beyond recognition. In fact, a greater percentage of his 1930s homes in Los Angeles remain intact than his more recent La Jolla work. Only on Dowling Drive, and some of the other more inland, less-disturbed locations, are intact examples extant. Disgraced by this second failure, any hope that Kesling might rehabilitate his reputation and record his achievements was gone. He had made few friends wherever he practiced. Kesling's own recollections were never recorded. After his death, his widow, believing that his work would never be of interest, destroyed his notes and records. Despite this anonymity, Kesling lives in the subconscious of countless Southern Californians who have seen his noteworthy buildings sprinkled throughout their cities.

Kesling Family Archive

CHAPTER 4

KESLING'S DESIGN

Central to Kesling's success was his ability to incorporate advancements in knowledge with changes in aesthetics. Early in his career he produced commendable Spanish and Tudor homes. He made his greatest mark with his Streamline designs of the 1930s but he also constructed notable modern buildings during and after the Second World War that reflected the aesthetic of the day. Self-taught, Kesling had developed his own independent theories and was open to their continuing evolution. Though this review will look at each era and his more important homes separately, a clear appreciation should emerge of the extent of Kesling's work and the range of his abilities.

Most Streamline buildings were large institutional projects like the Coca-Cola building, Jefferson High School, the Academy Theater, and the Pan Pacific Auditorium. Public acceptance of the style largely ended at the homestead threshold. It was one thing to work in a Streamline factory, school, or office building; it was another to actually live in such a home. Kesling's edge was making his Streamline homes less austere and building them at a budget within reach of the common homebuyer. His homes offered a kind of Streamline Populism perfect for the time. Kesling understood the special appeal of Streamline's transportation theme to Angelinos. By his placement of balconies and upstairs windows, both the model home and the Johnstone house, among many others, resemble steamship bridges. The Beery house, with its winged floor plan, hovering pergolas, and skyward-looking clearstory windows, invokes a flight aesthetic that indulged the clients love of flying. A canopy over the driveway of the

Johnstone house extends out like a wing or vapor trail. Enhancing this image were horizontal, chrome bands and light fixtures, steel-framed windows and disappearing pocket-doors, common to almost all of Kesling's homes.

It is not difficult to identify a Kesling-designed Streamline home. Several signature features and characteristics are evident in various combinations in all his projects. Two features, usually visible from the street, are common to every Kesling home: the decorative parapet band and, more importantly, the custom, horizontal casement windows. As a decorative feature, Kesling attached 2 x 10 lumber to the wood frame within the top eighteen inches of his parapets. Once the house was stuccoed, the resulting eleven-inch high, two-inch thick raised bands wrapping completely around the buildings accentuated its horizontal emphasis. Kesling was not the only builder to add this feature, but his bands were unique in their size, shape, and ubiquity. On many of the homes these bands were set in relation to canopies, which made the bands themselves often appear to be planes slicing completely through the buildings. As important as this feature is in identifying his work, Kesling's windows are definitive. Almost always placed at the corner of his rooms, the windowpanes always had more width than height. Those windows facing the street were opaque, usually placed high and used more sparingly for privacy, while the back of the house contained walls of glass framing a view, such as a garden. Though built to look machine-made and prefabricated, his windows were custom made on-site. In a typical large bank of windows, containing perhaps 16 panes or more,

Left: The model home (1935) was placed close to the street to make maximum use of its steep site.

it was common for every pane to be of a slightly different size. As a first step, galvanized sheet metal was attached along the top as flashing and extended out about two inches to act as a rain visor, and along the bottom of the window frame as a sill with the same two-inch visor. On any window comprising more than two horizontal panes, steel plates were welded to the end of 1 1/2-inch diameter pipes cut to length, and then set vertically into place at the window pane joints as integral parts of the houses' framing. At that point, one-inch T-bar and L-bar were welded into a grid that set into the window opening and screwed to the vertical pipes. Hinged windows were used sparingly, as the budget allowed. Finally, the glass panes were cut to size and easily glazed into the steel frames. All these steps were undertaken on-site. Using rectangular panes of almost "golden" proportions, Kesling enjoyed nearly unlimited variations of size and shape. Some of his window units were as wide as seven uninterrupted panes stretching over eighteen feet and reaching over seven feet (five panes) high. The same steel piping that formed the backbone of his windows reappear elsewhere in his houses most notably as railing for his many decks and stairs. To further the horizontal theme of his designs, these railings were kept low with a minimum of vertical and horizontal members. Other uses for the piping included structural support for overhangs or canopies; inside, these pipes

Inset: Kesling almost always surrounded his chimneys with windows. In the Campbell house (1936), the curving chimney above the mantle evokes both streamline and southwestern influence. Left: Though Kesling adopted the modern practice of placing the front door entering directly into the living area, he often placed a wall for privacy and/or a seating alcove around a corner. The Hough house (1935) in Silverlake has both. Note the aluminum tiles surrounding the fireplace.

Photos by David Sadofsky

49

were commonly used as staircase handrails, fireplace mantle supports, or room partition supports. Kesling took every opportunity to further the illusion of a modern, steel-frame house. He recognized the coming trend of steel-frame construction and embraced the style if not the complete substance.

Common interior features of Kesling's Streamline homes were built-in furniture and cabinetry. To efficiently use his limited space, Kesling almost always installed built-in seating and shelving in his living rooms. Most often these seats were placed on the same wall as the front door, with a separating partition facing across the living room and toward the invariable wall of windows. Unlike other Streamline builders, Kesling sometimes used fine wood veneers to cover his built-ins. These built-ins were given a machine-like, high gloss and often incorporated curving shapes. Simple and inexpensive, his cabinetry and shelving appeared throughout all of his houses. Made of simple, three-quarter-inch plywood with either very simple hardware or no hardware at all, they were largely designed to blend smoothly into a room. Kesling's light fixtures showed remarkable simplicity and sophistication. Using the same T-bar with which he assembled his windows, he usually miter-cut simple rectangular shapes, chromed or painted them, and fitted the lenses with milk glass or textured glass. Occasionally wood cut and painted to resemble steel was used to save time and money. These fixtures were mounted in holes in the ceiling with incandescent bulbs set inside. In public rooms Kesling would sometimes stack several such chromed rectangles into a more elaborate arrangement. These lights could also be mounted on walls or on both walls and ceiling where they meet. In some instances, the wood frame of the homes could be seen behind the lens when lit. Kesling also employed indirect lighting, emanating from soffits that he built in his living rooms and bedrooms.

Right: The Campbell house's lightweight, living-room shelves illustrate Kesling's skill in simple effective carpentry design and execution.

David Sadofsky

The Rivero house (1936) offers a good example of the deeper, larger tubs Kesling preferred to create with tile rather than the enamel iron tubs that were common.

David Sadofsky

Unlike many designers of the 1930s (modern or otherwise) who gave their baths little consideration, Kesling designed baths that were far more than afterthoughts. Their most interesting features were his bathtubs. Eschewing a typical, and seemingly more cost-effective, cast-iron enamel tub, Kesling chose to construct deep, oversized tubs out of ceramic tile. With a slight incline at the back and vertical on the other three sides, his baths looked something like a Japanese soaking tub. Under one house he added a twelve-by-ten-foot, four-foot-deep tile swimming pool which Kesling referred to as a "Roman bath." Unlike typical tile that is laid in an offset, interlocking pattern, Kesling laid his tile in perfect alignment, so the grout-lines became extended, unbroken vertical and horizontal lines. There is some evidence that Kesling tried linoleum countertops on some projects. As linoleum proved unsatisfactory, all of it was eventually replaced, some within months, others several years later. Therefore, it is not completely clear where Kesling's tile design begins and ends on many of his projects. His sink areas were often lit by chrome-plated, rectangular lights installed in ceilings lowered over the sink. Sometimes these lights wrapped around this soffit to light both the sink area and the general room area. Often, modest sink areas were surrounded by three-faceted mirrors, two of which open to reveal a medicine cabinet. A few bathrooms had striking vanities with rounded cabinetry. Conversely, some were extremely utilitarian and spare. The choices of material (tile, chrome, linoleum, and glass) and design (simple and bare) were guided by a modern desire for antiseptic cleanliness. Nearly all of Kesling's bathrooms enjoyed light and fresh air from large windows of textured glass.

Kesling continued this philosophy in his kitchens. Employing the same materials as his baths, they were compact, and efficient.

They were also as bright and windowed as any room he designed. Every sink was placed below a window and every kitchen offered a work counter under a window. In all but a few homes, he included some sort of breakfast nook, ranging in size from a separate room with a built-in bench and table, to (more often) a simple countertop across a small space with room for one or perhaps two chairs. This seating was always surrounded by glass and, if it was the simple countertop arrangement, the diner would be facing a picture window.

Kesling's doors were also distinctive. At least nine of his houses featured pocket-doors. The front doors were often made of mahogany, sometimes trimmed with chrome strips as guiding. Pocket-doors to the backyard were often glass with wood framing to match the horizontal lines of the windows. Kesling's doors were never centered if he could avoid it. Depending on the budget, interior doors ranged from those made of inexpensive pine or plywood shaped into completely flat slabs, to those constructed of luxurious wood such as birch or mahogany. Between many common spaces, doors were eliminated altogether.

The evolution of Kesling's floor plans is quite interesting. In his first few homes, he did not fully reject the traditional assumptions about a home's basic layout. His model home hedged on the modernist precept of an open floor plan by separating the front door from the living room with a built-in, bookcase room divider and a curtain, and separating the living and dining rooms with a glass partition. It was as if Kesling didn't quite have the courage to create a fully open interior. The Johnstone house also has a separate, formal entry with a classic, central staircase and separate living and dining rooms. It is reasonable to wonder if Kesling toned down these early projects as insurance against building a home that wouldn't sell. By the time he designed his

David Sadofsky

Wooden discs mounted as drawer-pulls and door handles and large graphic circles routed from plywood panels remake the otherwise simple guest-bath vanity of the Skinner House (1936).

fourth Streamline project, entryways were incorporated into the living room and the dining room was simply an area intimately connected to this living room.

Ironically, Kesling erected all these groundbreaking Streamline designs with few new techniques or materials. Too early to employ the coming materials of modern construction, Kesling's deft use of the materials available invoked the promise of the future through modern design. The construction remained the basic, hand-troweled stucco on wood frame as practiced in Los Angeles for generations. Steel was not integral to the structure. The roofs appeared flat, but actually sloped behind parapets. Kesling's windows looked like precision pieces produced on an assembly line; in reality, they were cut and fit on sight. The tiles (ceramic and aluminum) were boldly colored and laid in modern patterns and the wood on the floors, doors, and built-ins were finished to an almost unnatural gloss. His machine-made look was almost completely handmade. Kesling spoke the vernacular of the style, yet employed many of the materials and construction techniques used for decades.

When Kesling resumed his career in 1939, he did not return to Streamline design. His designs evidence a transition toward what would come to be known as post-modern. His wartime projects solidified his philosophy of combining compact and economic design with new materials and techniques. When the same designs that were well received by the critics of *Arts+Architecture*, were erected in La Jolla during the postwar housing shortage, they were derided by the *Los Angeles Times* as "Kesling's Kozy Kowsheds." In fact, both his wartime and postwar compact buildings were remarkably well designed, livable, and affordable. Built on a poured slab with three-quarter-inch walls framed by 2 x 4s and a simple plywood roof on 2 x 6 runners, Kesling's homes relied on layout and windows for livability. An open floor plan with multipurpose rooms sided by large windows was the key. As materials were so difficult to obtain, most windows did not open and were simply tacked into place with wood moldings used as stops. Others were floor-to-ceiling and slid aside to allow egress to the backyard. The extreme lightness of this construction brought derision from some, but buyers were attracted; fourteen such homes were eventually built. Many residents have happily remained in these homes for decades. Once again, Kesling was aiming for the mid-level market rather than the high-end segment to which so many modernists catered. Building such economical structures in a city such as La Jolla invited confrontation and contributed to his eventual downfall. Kesling leveraged this experience to lucratively build even less expensive and less interesting homes in the Mira Mesa area of San Diego. These homes did nothing to contribute to Kesling's body of work except provide the income to enable him to accept some very interesting commissions. Concurrently with these projects, Kesling resumed custom home construction for the third time. His transition to post-modern style complete, he quickly reestablished himself as a creative force worthy of note. His critical recognition, local and national, actually matched his considerable financial success. Much had changed in the seven years since his last Streamline home. Much had also remained. Kesling still emphasized economy, configuring his homes with efficient open floor plans and employing windows to maximize sunlight and a feeling of space. His changes included a semi-post and beam construction, pitched roofs with an exposed structure, and the abandonment of steel or any other metal as a material. From the more-modest Everett and King houses to the spectacular $40,000 McConnell house, Kesling trademarks are apparent to the well-versed student.

William Kesling was remarkable for both his talent and his versatility. Over more than forty years he brought his design skills to modern architecture and grew and adapted as it progressed from International style through the post-war era.

Left: Kesling's La Jolla project (1947) was a perfect answer to the postwar housing shortage.

Julius Shulman

THE MODEL HOME

With his model home, Kesling boldly announced his talent as a modern designer and builder, and immediately established himself as a player in Los Angeles' modern movement. Though it might initially appear otherwise, the site was ideal for Kesling's purposes. On the one hand it was on a narrow street, without sidewalks or lights. The lot was extremely steep, with the only potential building area pushed right up against the street. On the other hand, Silverlake was fast becoming a center of modern design and the lot Kesling chose hung out over the canyon with a commanding view. It was clearly visible to anyone who traveled Silverlake Boulevard. The lack of amenities and steep slope of the lot kept the land price down, which was paramount since Kesling built this house with his own meager funds. To this day, the house remains a dramatic jewel. Sited up close to the street with a little front yard, it has a very low street-side profile, with the chimney barely rising above the roofline. The rectangular windows along the front are mostly placed high for privacy from street traffic. The lines created by the eaves over the entry and front bedroom are extended as a ten-inch-high band, which wraps around nearly the entire house. The window blinds and

Left: In the Model Home (1935) Kesling used every opportunity to accentuate the horizontal—even the window blinds and the garage doors. Note how the chimney is unobtrusive and dangerously low, venting close to the roof.

57

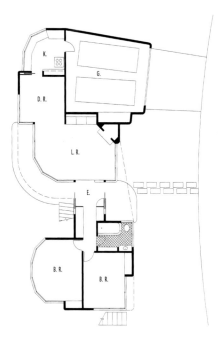

Left: Mahogany veneers on the walls and built-ins continue the tone set in the entry.

David Sadofsky

Left: The entryway features mahogany doors and built-ins and a cork floor. This is one of only a few separate entryways Kesling built. Note the heat register below the bookshelf. Right: Contrasting with the front façade the hillside slope creates a more vertical feeling in the back.

garage door combine with these features to add to the horizontal emphasis. The front door is a pocket-door, which opens onto a small, central entry. From this tiny space much about Kesling's designs can be learned. The inside of the front door and two wonderful built-ins are veneered in mahogany. The floor is cork. The fixtures are chrome plated. Another glass pocket-door just eight feet opposite the front door brings the canyon view below into the house. When both the doors are opened, the indoor-outdoor aspects Philip Lovell championed are evident. In what may have been a concession to more traditional sensibilities, a curtain originally separated the entry from the living room. The living room features a fireplace and built-in seating area paneled in more mahogany. An enormous, four-faceted window wraps entirely around the southwest corner of the room from knee height to ceiling. Kesling knew that getting the most from a small area was key to keeping down costs, and these windows give the rooms of this compact house a feeling of space and light far greater than their size. The dining room was partially separated from the living room by a glass partition. Another pocket-door leads to the kitchen. A built-in sideboard features marbleized cork facing. To the left of the entry, down a short, cork-floored hall are the bedrooms and bath. The eight-faceted, master bedroom enjoys the same 180-degree canyon view as the living room. These two rooms look across to each other. Below the main floor, through a separate entrance, is a studio apartment that the Keslings initially used as their office. Like many of Kesling's and other Depression era projects, this space originally was only minimally finished—the assumption being that this work would be completed when better times returned.

Julius Shulman

JOHNSTONE HOUSE

Dr. Harry C. Johnstone ambitiously contracted Kesling for the design and construction (on speculation) of a larger, 2,300-square-foot home in the more-affluent Los Feliz district, on a lot costing a relatively expensive $350. That he had enough confidence in Kesling's work to build such a large home during such dire economic times is a tribute to both Kesling's work and his salesmanship. The house repeats many of the features that worked so well on the model home. It is set well towards the front of the lot to maximize backyard space. Windows facing the street are placed high to increase privacy and walls facing the rear are nearly all glass. Like the model home, a second, large, windowed pocket-door in the entry draws the outside garden into the interior space. In this house, Kesling makes some interesting concessions to more traditional design. In terms of the layout, Kesling made the dining room a separate, formal room rather than following the modern, space-saving norm of incorporating such a space into the living area. This house also had a separate entry hall, instead of a front door entering directly into the living room. A short hallway downstairs and a landing and hall upstairs seemed counter to Kesling's desire to eliminate such wasted space in his compact designs. Strikingly, the garage was placed behind the house at the rear of the lot rather than on the

Left: The Johnstone house (1935) was built by Kesling in Los Feliz, for a speculator who then could not sell the home for over two years.

Photos by David Sadofsky

Above: One of few staircases not finished in magnasite. The chrome rails and light are less typical. The tile was originally laid on the upstairs balcony and was salvaged and reused during restoration.
Left: The living room shows how Kesling maximized windows and views that were private and minimized those facing the street. The south wall continues 14 feet into the backyard further shielding the living room from the sun.

street, as might be expected from such a proponent of the transportation vernacular. All four of these deviations from Kesling's norm required extra space, materials, and costs at a time when few could afford any extras. Some of the cosmetic features also differed from what might be expected from Kesling. As with only a few other early Kesling homes, the living room ceiling was trimmed with a relief more decorative than would seem his taste. In another seemingly un-modern touch, flowerboxes were built into both front windows. The breakfast nook was a separate room from the kitchen and both it and the dining room were outfitted with foot buzzers to call domestic help. This last feature makes it clear that this house was not designed for the middle-class market. It certainly did not suggest a "socialist architecture," as some had branded the International style. These differences may imply a possible nervousness on behalf of Dr. Johnstone concerning the salability of his speculation. Perhaps he felt that, in such a neighborhood, certain concessions to the tastes and sensibilities of the neighbors were wise.

Despite these influences, the Johnstone house is one of Los Angeles' best examples of Streamline residential architecture. The facade displays some of Kesling's best use of masses and shapes. With all its south-facing corners rounded and most of its north-facing corners squared, a cantilever extending out north over the driveway like a vapor trail, shapes that look somewhat like smokestacks and a bridge-like balcony, to the imaginative, the house suggests the bridge of a steamship heading south. Unlike Kesling's many hillside houses, where massing is often dictated by the topography of the site, the Johnstone house's massing was unrestricted by such concerns. Without this restriction, Kesling used light and sightlines to dictate the placement of his rooms, and windows that allowed views from every direction while retaining absolute privacy. As Lovell would have recommended, every bedroom offered windows on three sides, and every bathroom offered windows on two sides. By setting the house forward and completely across the width of the lot, the back 90 feet of lot depth was left for a private yard. The south wall of the living room extended out into the back yard, further blurring the distinction between indoor and outdoor and adding to privacy. From the moment visitors reached the mahogany veneered front pocket-door with its one-way glass window, they knew they were somewhere new. Before one even passed through the front door the backyard came into view through the large, glass pocket-door opposite. On the left an "s" shaped wall led the eye to the living room and the outdoors beyond. To the immediate right above the door was a three-dimensional, rectangular box of chrome and milk-glass set on the wall to light the entryway. The stairway and landing in this entry had chrome railings identical to what one would expect at the local plunge. The tiles now in the entryway were originally laid on the upstairs balcony, and re-laid during major renovation in 1986. The living room was dominated by a sculptural fireplace. Placed at a prominent corner, it featured a curved mantle trimmed with chrome. The hearth was lined with a thin, horizontal, terra cotta glazed brick. Custom andirons of cast aluminum and an ash guard made of aluminum and copper-plated steel added to the machine-like feeling. The living room itself was perhaps Kesling's largest-scale living room. Although he built other Streamline rooms that were larger, they were multipurpose; this was the largest single-use room. As for Dr. Johnstone, his fears were borne out when he found himself unable to sell the house and it remained vacant and unsold for about two years. Kesling's legal problems were probably the primary reason; or perhaps Kesling's Streamline structures were just too daring among the Spanish, Georgian, and Tudor homes of Los Feliz.

Left: Rear Johnstone house.

BEERY HOUSE

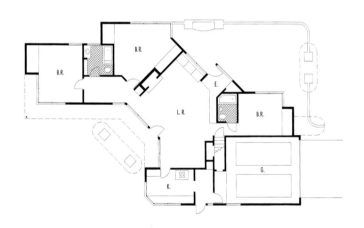

In Wallace Beery, Kesling found the ideal client. As Beery already occupied a Beverly Hills mansion, this second West Hollywood home would be located near the studio where he worked. It was a place where he could retreat for privacy during filming and entertain or accommodate friends and industry figures. Although a minor luxury to America's highest earning male star, the $3.50 per-square-foot budget was the most generous Kesling would enjoy. However, their shared aesthetic was far more important than Beery's funds. Kesling's bold Streamline designs spoke to Beery's love of aircraft and flying. Wing-like pergola gates at the front of the house and another patio-shade pergola in the back combined with Kesling's clearstory and casement

Left: In Wallace Beery, Kesling had one of his most daring clients and he responded with one of his most flamboyant designs.

Photos by David Sadofsky

Above: Compact but well detailed this bath features a built-in light, towel rack, and cabinet. Built primarily for entertaining, neither bath was ensuite—instead both had direct access to the public rooms. Left: Transom windows, cantilevering, and a deceptive shape can give an illusion that confuses indoors with outdoors.

David Sadofsky

windows to give the appearance of perhaps a small air terminal. Luxuries were also added. The front gates opened to a private courtyard containing a fountain with a top that matched the pergolas. This is Kesling's only known water feature, although he did install a ten-by-ten-foot "Roman bath" below the Hunter house. Among the other luxuries was a ten-foot ceiling in the living/dining room with clearstory windows looking skyward, and a rooftop sundeck accessed by a hidden stairway. Entertaining was the home's primary purpose and the layout reflected this. The living and dining rooms shared one space to allow maximum flexibility as never before. This space enjoyed built-in seating, a multicolored flagstone fireplace, and a view across the backyard to a large barbeque grill of the same stone. This view was through a bank of Kesling's windows that played an interesting trick on the eye. With the pergola on the patio so close to the house and the way the window bank cut into the house, for a moment it would almost appear that the outside was inside and vice versa. To facilitate entertaining, both baths were directly accessible from the living room area; neither were en suite. Though relatively small, these baths were well appointed with typical Kesling features. None of the bedrooms were large and even the master bedroom was relatively compact, implying Beery probably intended this home for people other than himself.

It seems clear that if Kesling had not encountered his legal and financial difficulties, this house, with its famous client and flamboyant style, would have propelled Kesling to even greater heights.

Right: Wallace Beery was Hollywood's top box office earner in 1934. His love of airplanes and flying translated into a love of Kesling's designs. Left: The airplane imagery of the front gateway is just one evocation of the theme. Courtesy MGM.

VErNON HOUsE

Some of the lore of this house also relates to its proximity and association to a nearby studio. Built in the Valley Village neighborhood of the San Fernando Valley, it was close to Warner Bros. Studio and was purportedly used for informal entertainment and as a guesthouse for the studio. The present owner continues this tradition with frequent gatherings largely attended by members of the art and entertainment communities. Furnished with an eclectic mix of items and art dating from the 1930s to the present, it is remarkable how well the house serves as a stage for the pieces. This is the first house Kesling built on a lot large enough to allow for an ample front yard. It featured a front picture window, which would be too exposed without the available setback. In these regards it could be considered Kesling's only "suburban" house. The added lot width allowed Kesling to further emphasize the

Left: Vernon House, Valley Village, North Hollywood, (1936). Left: From the back, the transom windows are apparent just above the roofline.

horizontal orientation of the building with long lines forming eaves and canopies. As in the Adams home and others, a faceted light is set into a curving wall separating the garage from the entry. Kesling repeats the clearstory windows he used so successfully in the Beery house. In the living room they are placed over the front window and door, facing north, and over the rear windows and doors, facing south and west. These windows, especially at the south and west, pour sunlight into the living room. Like the Johnstone house, a soffit with indirect lighting crosses along one wall. A somewhat free-form fireplace divides the living and dining areas. A windowed pocket-door leads to the kitchen. The back of the house has no less than 11 separate vertical planes from side to side. The back porch resembles a stage. An unusual single windowpane is placed directly below this porch in the unfinished, half-basement. Every public room and the master bedroom has ample windows looking onto the large back yard. The open layout and roomy situation of the house support the contention that the home was built primarily for entertainment.

Right: The Vernon house, was built on one of Kesling's larger, more level lots. It uses front and back walls of windows, with transoms, to bring in the sky.

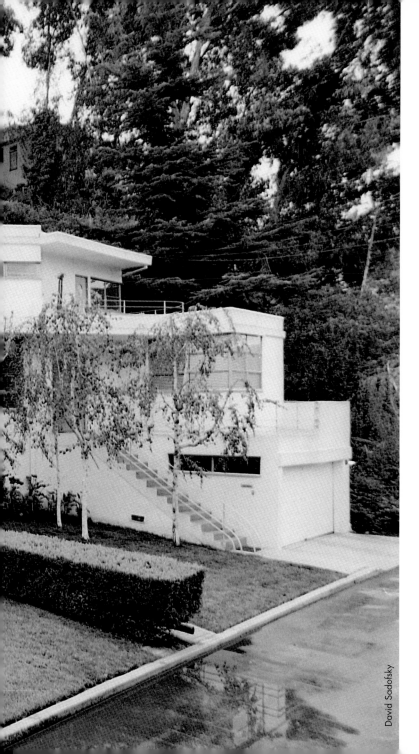

David Sadofsky

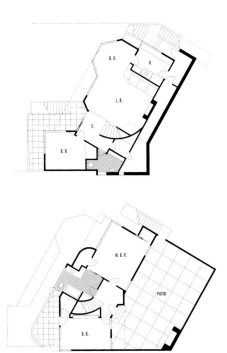

SKINNER HOUSE

Left: Though built almost a year apart, these two Keslings in Silverlake are placed as if planned together.

David Sadofsky

In the Skinner house Kesling returned to an up-slope lot next to his Vanderpool house, a siting that suited his designs well. As both the Vanderpool and Skinner homes were set at an angle with windows placed as if one knew what was going up next door, it can only be assumed that Kesling intended this pair all along. With the model home just down the block, the possibilities of a Streamline neighborhood could be glimpsed.

The up-sloping lot played to Kesling's affinity for terraces and dramatic interior spaces. After climbing a flight of stairs with a flat steel banister to the front porch balcony and entering the portholed pocket-door, the visitor was greeted by a curving magnasite stairway with a graceful banister of chromed flat steel and pipe. Kesling used magnasite on almost all his stairs. A large chrome steel pole seems to support this stairway opening. Like his other homes at this time, entry was into a living room

Left: In the Skinner house (1936) rich wood veneers of mahogany and cork, brought a feeling of warmth and luxury to a style often perceived by the public as antiseptic and austere.

Above: The same circular theme continues with the kitchen cabinetry—even the range.
Left: Kesling's built-ins were among his signature features and the Skinner house in Silverlake contains the best preserved examples as in this upstairs library case.

Photos by David Sadofsky

83

David Sadofsky

featuring a mahogany-paneled fireplace mantle, built-in seating, storage, and shelves. Windows banked the entire street side.

The cabinets throughout the house were more stylized than most, but still offer the best remaining examples of his work. Kesling normally designed and built very simple, inexpensive cabinets with chrome hardware. With this house he took his simple design and added geometry. Continuing the circular theme begun with the porthole in the front door (and repeated in the upstairs balcony and back doors), he adorned nearly every piece with circles. Circles were routed out of cabinet faces, wooden discs were fashioned into handles and pulls, and three mirrored circles were set into the master bath's cabinetry.

Kesling always gave his baths special attention. At 100 square feet, the master bath in the Skinner house may have been his most grand. Nine feet of high windows wrapped around the exterior. A long, horizontal vanity light over the mirror replicated the window's shape. A chrome-trimmed pocket-door separated the bath from the master bedroom.

With the Skinner house, Kesling progressed further in his unique Streamline direction. Adding a few more decorative features and a few more luxuries, he was solidifying a Southern California version of Streamline that largely abandoned the axioms of the International style. The Skinner house is a prime example.

Left: The master bath in the Skinner house is perhaps the most luxurious Kesling built.

David Sadofsky

ADAMS HOUSE

Begun in fall 1936, the Adams house displayed many of Kesling's characteristic features and refinements in a small project. Placed on another steep, down-sloping lot on a narrow street without sidewalks, the compact front facade used simple Kesling features to create an inviting public face. A semicircular light was mounted between the garage and the entry area. A simple, three-pane window brought sunlight to the stairwell and a high curved window wrapped from the front door to the fireplace. Kesling's use of space was even more efficient than with previous projects. As with so many of his homes, immediately upon entry visitors were greeted by large windows facing the canyon. A windowed door opened to a viewing deck outside. A built-in seating area to the left followed the contours of the room nearly to the fireplace. Matching, inset bookshelves framed the simplest of hearths. The stairway doubled back almost behind the front door. In the dining area, the sideboard

Left: The Adams house (1935), built close to the street on a narrow, steep lot, again uses Kesling's window placement to maximize both light and privacy.

87

David Sadofsky

used sheet metal curved into a rounded end to tie the living and dining areas together. Downstairs, the shape and size of the bedrooms were consistent with his other homes, as were the ample windows. A relatively large bath and dressing room stood out as unusual for Kesling's designs. Common to many Kesling (and other Depression era) projects, was the inclusion of unfinished space, presumably waiting to be completed in better times.

This home was unique in that it was the only Streamline home in which the original, Kesling-drawn floor plans survive. Not only do they evidence Kesling's abilities, they are the only true, reliable record of exactly what Kesling intended. For example, there has been a long-running debate about the extent of his use of tile in kitchens and baths. Many people (including the author) have felt that he may have experimented with linoleum counter-tops, etc. Building records often show separate permits for tiling after initial construction, which suggests that retrofitting occurred. The floorplans of the Adams house clearly show that tile was intended for all these countertops from the outset. They also demonstrate how the final product did not completely match his intentions, whether it is the minor difference in the shape and size of the dining room buffet, or more important compromises such as the number of operable windows. How much that related to his financial problems cannot be determined.

Left: In the living room Kesling uses simple shelves to create an elegant fireplace.

David Sadofsky

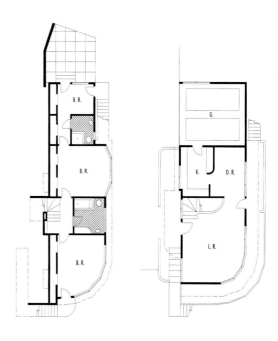

RIVERO HOUSE

Left: On a difficult site, even by Kesling's standards, all windows of the Rivero house (1936) aim at the city view.

Photos by David Sadofsky

A small cottage with an enormous view, it was never enjoyed by the original clients, due to tragedy. As one of Kesling's later projects, the Rivero house showed his continued, and even improved, understanding of how to economize space and materials. At the time of this writing, it is among the best preserved and restored of Kesling's Streamline homes. On a narrow lot, the steepest with which Kesling had yet worked, off a shared driveway, he perched this jewel box of a home. Large, faceted windows (one above the other) facing a view sweeping from the ocean to downtown, evoke the idea of a control tower or a steamship bridge. Just as his other homes brought their backyard gardens or canyons into their living spaces, this house brought

Inset: Kesling used magnasite on nearly every interior stairway he built. In the Rivero home in West Hollywood, he made the rails of the same steel as his window frames and balcony railings. Left: The Rivero House is another example of how Kesling brought the outside into his small spaces to create a very open and spacious atmosphere.

Los Angeles into its space. Despite its relatively small rooms, the feeling of space and the urge to live both indoors and outdoors predominate. Once again, his design and construction skills placed affordable housing on an otherwise uneconomical site.

All the features of Kesling's larger homes are present here in smaller, simpler forms. From the front, the decorative band and canopy provide the horizontal emphasis. Elevated windows add light with privacy to the living room. Both the dramatic, windowed stairwell and the front door seem of diminutive scale. No other Kesling house utilizes its available space so fully. The front door entry and the upstairs landing are incorporated into the living room. With the limitations of the site, even the semblance of a front yard is abandoned. Every Kesling home possessed at least one unique feature. The most interesting, original aspect of this home is the faceting used on the curves of the balcony and eave. The curve, and the ability to use it, was basic to Streamline design. Kesling's wraparound windows were faceted by necessity, but his stuccoed, horizontal planes were always rounded. Here his balcony, overhang, and railings all mirror the window facets.

The single, downstairs bathroom is compact, yet comfortable, serving as both the bedroom bath and guest bath. High windows bring light and a green view into the space. The best remaining example of the type of bathtubs Kesling installed in nearly all his homes is found here. The tub is perhaps 16 inches deep; the back has a slight incline to lie against. The influence of the Japanese soaking tub is apparent. The ceiling space over the bath was not tiled. Instead, one-inch wooden slats with half-inch spaces in between—reminiscent of the pallets often used as flooring in a Japanese bath—concealed this cavity and allowed steam to rise out of the bath.

Left: Rear of Rivero House.

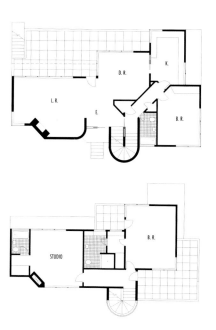

ULM HOUJE

The Ulm house is particularly interesting because of its late groundbreaking one month after Kesling had pled guilty and agreed to cease building. A look at the original building permit does not list any contractor, but the initials WPK appear as a notation over the then-extravagant stated project value of $7,500. Even without this little clue, one look confirms that this house is a Kesling design, if not also Kesling construction. All of his trademark materials and design elements are evident: his

Left: The Ulm house (1937) was built on a more gentle slope which allowed Kesling to design generous terraces and balconies.

Photos by David Sadofsky

open layout, windows, facades, and balconies. Kesling used glass block (in a high, curving wall) for the first time here. At 2,150 square feet, this house was nearly as large and, in many ways, more luxurious than the nearby Johnstone house. Comparing these two homes shows just how far Kesling progressed into uncompromised modernism.

Finished true to Kesling's plans, this house is again set close to the street to maximize private outdoor space and take advantage of its sloping lot. With a generous use of balconies, he created a pleasant terraced effect that plays well on the site—another example of Kesling's "machine in the garden." Rather than sloping directly up or down from the street, as did his previous houses, this lot also sloped laterally from left to right. Kesling used this slope to tuck the garage under the house and create a larger, level living space above. Front windows were again placed for privacy, and a stout chimney was turned to a 45-degree angle. As with many other Kesling homes, upon climbing the front stairs and entering through the pocket-door the visitor is greeted by an open floor plan and large windows along the entire rear, facing the backyard. Balconies run along nearly every wall that faces the rear yard. An interesting, narrow hall slices across the downstairs in a clever way. Off this hall is a surprisingly utilitarian bathroom for such an otherwise luxurious home. A curving, magnasite main stairway, lit by a glass-block wall, descends beside the front door. Commodious upstairs bedroom, bath, and studio spaces (with another long balcony) complete the layout.

Above: Surprisingly, this is the only Kesling in which the original use of glass block is documented. The curved wall of the stairway here dominates the house both inside and outside.

EPILOGUE

Near the end of his career, William Kesling estimated that, between 1922 and 1962, he had constructed over 3,500 structures. Yet, unlike many of his less productive, more famous peers, he remains nearly unknown after decades. In greater Los Angeles, architectural academics and devotees of modern architecture may have been familiar with Kesling's buildings, but, invariably, they were unacquainted with his name. The same is true in the San Diego area. Misattribution of his work is common. Sensational rumors became part of his obscure legacy. Even among his few admirers, an uneasy doubt persists.

Yet, today, Kesling's recognition is beginning to grow among students of modern architecture and his Streamline homes are becoming local landmarks. His work is being understood for the ground it broke, both architecturally and socially, while his difficulties are quickly fading from memory. Facts have been unearthed and rumors have been dispelled. With fifty years perspective, Kesling is now rightfully being judged for his designs and production rather than his poor business acumen.

In his forward to this book, David Gebhard stated, "(Streamline Moderne), like all vigorous architectural styles, arrived on the wings of fashion and left the same way." The popularity of Kesling's buildings declined rapidly. Within a few years his Streamline homes were out of favor both commercially and stylistically. For many years thereafter his Streamline buildings were ignored. As a result, his modern structures, which required extra care and maintenance, generally received just the opposite. In the beach communities of San Diego, intact Kesling homes are rare for a different reason. Few of his modest, postwar homes remain as they were mostly built on what are now very desirable lots in La Jolla. As is the sad case in too many California beach communities, many of the custom homes he built there have been altered, razed, expanded and man-sionized beyond recognition.

Though the majority of Kesling's work no longer exists, enough examples remain to offer a representative sample of his work. One by one, Kesling's remaining Streamline homes are being rediscovered and restored. Although some continue their neglected decline, more are returned to past glory every year. The restoration effort and expense to which some homeowners have gone is truly remarkable and an undiluted civic service. For the first time in decades "pride in ownership" would be an apt description for the condition of many of his homes. In San

Diego, and particularly La Jolla, where he built the most homes, those that retain their postwar Kesling character are receiving added attention. On Dowling Street, perhaps a dozen of the homes that the *Los Angeles Times* dubbed "Keslings Kozy Kowsheds," remain in nearly original condition. The owners have generally retained their homes' original character without knowing of Kesling, but simply because they appreciate the design.

The quality and breadth of Kesling's work cannot be denied. By looking at his career in its totality, it is clear that he was indeed an important figure in the progression of Southern California's modern built environment. The time has come that he be properly recognized.

A CHRONOLOGICAL LISTING OF PROJECTS

1) The Model Home, Easterly Terrace, Silverlake:
Completed in 1935 this 1242 sq. ft. home was Kesling's first Streamline home and was built within a budget of $3,600.

2) Johnstone House, Lowry Road, Los Feliz:
Built in 1935, this home was among his largest Streamline homes at 2731 sq. ft. Its $7,500 budget was also large by Kesling's standards.

3) Hough House, Effie Street, Silverlake:
Built in 1935, this 1125 sq. ft. home cost $3,500.

4) Estes House, Broadlawn Drive, Studio City:
Completed in 1936, this 1311 sq. ft. home was Kesling's first outside the Silverlake/Los Feliz area. Its budget was $2,500.

5) Kesling Modern Structures Offices, Silverlake Boulevard, Silverlake:
Clearly, the $1,500 budget reflects the economies he enjoyed building this 2942 sq. ft. office for Kesling Modern Structures in 1936.

6) Collins House, Silverwood Terrace, Silverlake:
Kesling returned to a steep hillside lot with this house built in 1936. At 1783 sq. ft. its budget was $4,000.

7) Vanderpool House, Easterly Terrace, Silverlake:
Returning to his favorite street in 1936 this was his first uphill lot. Its 1964 sq. ft. cost $4,000.

8) Vernon House, Otsego Street, Valley Village:
Built in 1936. The $4,500 budget was relatively high for its 1436 sq. ft. size. Like the Beery house, its layout suggests entertaining.

9) Hunter House, Fanning Street, Silverlake:
From 1936, a larger 1710 sq. ft. down-slope home, costing $3,590.

10) Campbell House, Webster Avenue:
This compact 1119 sq. ft. home, built in 1936, had a generous budget of $3,500.

11) Evans Triplex, Rendell Place, Silverlake:
In 1936 Kesling created this terrific triplex stacked up a sloping lot. Aggregating approximately 2700 sq. ft., it was budgeted at $6,500.

12) Dill House, Vista del Monte, Van Nuys:
The $4,000 budget seems high for this 1150 sq. ft. home built far from Kesling's other projects in 1936.

13) Beery House, Martel, West Los Angeles:
In 1936 Kesling went wild with this 1404 sq. ft. home budgeted at $5,000 for the deep-pocketed movie star.

14) Beery Duplex, Harper Avenue, West Hollywood:
In 1936, without waiting for his first project's completion, Beery had Kesling build this 2916 sq. ft. duplex with a $9,000 budget.

15) Skinner House, Easterly Terrace, Silverlake:
Completed at the end of 1936, this 2053 sq. ft. house, facing an earlier Kesling, was budgeted at $3,996. It is among the best preserved of Kesling's Streamline homes.

16) Adams House, Fernwood Avenue, Silverlake:
Completed in 1937, after his arrest but before his plea, this 1611 sq. ft., $3,990 home displays many of Kesling's refinements.

17) Rivero House, Miller Drive, West Hollywood:
Built in 1937, this 1349 sq. ft. small home has a large view. The $4,000 budget may have involved the costs associated with the very steep site.

18) Ulm House, Amesbury Road, Los Feliz:
Although his name does not appear on the building permit for this house from 1937, the layout, materials, and details make it evident this 2309 sq. ft. home was designed by Kesling. It was his last high-budget ($7,500) Streamline house.

19) Kibbe House, Easterly Terrace, Silverlake:
It is fitting that, in 1937, this, his last house in Silverlake, was built on the same block as his first Streamline house. This 1863 sq. ft. had a $5,800 budget.

20) Unknown client, Glen Holly Drive, Pasadena:
Finished in 1937, this house is clearly a Kesling design, but, due to his criminal conviction, it may not have been built under his supervision. Records do not survive.

21) Kaysor House, La Jolla:
In 1942 Kesling returned to custom design and construction and left Streamline design far behind.

22) Wartime Housing, 46th St. & Market, San Diego:
In 1942 these 100-649 sq. ft. units, built as housing for war production workers, received attention from *California Arts & Architecture* and launched an important time in Kesling's career.

23) Kozy Kowsheds, Dowling Drive, La Jolla:
Employing his wartime lessons, in 1946, Kesling began building these approximately 850 sq. ft. homes in inland La Jolla.

24) King House, Beaumont Street, La Jolla:
Kesling was smart to locate his practice in La Jolla. This custom home from 1947 is a good example of the design that propelled his career.

25) Gamson House, La Jolla:
In 1947 this 1196 sq. ft. home became *Better Homes & Gardens* Five Star Home #1711.

26) Ingle House, La Jolla:
Built in 1947, this inexpensive home showed how Kesling brought his low-cost building skills to custom construction to great success.

27) McConnell House, Spindrift Drive, La Jolla:
In 1947, *LIFE* magazine portrayed this $40,000 beachside home as a bachelor's paradise.

28) Borrego Springs Desert Club, Borrego Springs:
Built in 1948, this approximately 4800 sq. ft. steel clubhouse, boasts eleven consecutive 10 by 10-foot picture-windows tilted out to enhance the desert views. Kesling claimed to have built over 3,500 houses in the course of his career.

BIBLIOGRAPHY

1) Louis Adamic, *Laughing in the Jungle*, New York, Harper & Brothers, 1932

2) Bush, Donald J., *The Streamline Decade*, New York, George Braziller, Inc., 1975

3) Bel Geddes, Norman, *Horizons*, Boston, Little, Brown & Company, 1932

4) Betts, Hulda (with Gloria Larson), personal interview on July 17, 1999

5) *California Arts+Architecture, Modern Living Units*, November 1942, page 57

6) Chisholm, Joan and Lawrie, personal interviews on October 30 and December 11, 1999

7) Deardon's Department Store, *Home Furnishings Catalog*, Los Angeles, 1935

8) Forde-Murphy, Lucia, personal interview on December 12, 1999

9) Forrester, Russell, personal interview on December 11, 1999

10) Gebhard, David & Von Breton, Harriette, *L.A. in the 30's: 1931–1941*, New York, Peregrine Smith, Inc., 1975

11) *Streamline Moderne, Architecture*, American Institute of Architects, 1983

12) Greif, Martin, *Depression Modern: The Thirties Style in America*, New York, Universe Books, 1975

13) Grist, George A., *Probation Officer's Report*, Los Angeles County Department of Probation, 1937

14) Head, Ethel McCall, *Open Planning Brings the Outdoors In*, *Better Homes & Gardens*, July 1947, page 105

15) Hoye, Dan with Julius Shulman, *Profile: William Kesling*, Los Angeles Conservancy, 1984

16) *Illustrated Daily News, Contractor, Wife Indicted on Forgery Charges*, Los Angeles, December 9, 1936

17) Jeanneret, Charles Edouard (Le Corbusier), *Towards a New Architecture*, London, Architectural Press, 1927

18) Klein, Norman, *History of Forgetting: Los Angeles and the Erasure of Memory*, New York, Verso, 1997

19–21) Kesling, William Paul, *History of My Life, Resume of Our Present Trouble, A Resume Showing Our Method of Operating*, Los Angeles, 1937

22) *Resume of Qualifications of William Kesling*, La Jolla, 1964

23) Larson, Gloria, personal interviews on July 26, 1999 and January 23, 2000

24) *Life Visits a Cliffside House: Bachelor's Retreat Juts Over Surf*, *LIFE* magazine, November 3, 1947, page 154

25) City of Los Angeles Department of Building & Safety, *Applications for the Erection of a Building*, 27 issued separately between March 6, 1935 and May 21, 1937

26) Marshall, Dean, personal interviews on July 7, 1999 and October 29, 1999

27) Mayo, Morrow, *Los Angeles*, New York, Alfred A. Knopf, 1933

28) Mencken, H. L., *The New Architecture American Mercury Magazine*, February 1931

29) McWilliams, Carey, *Southern California: An Island on the Land*, New York, Duell, Sloan & Pearce, 1946

30) Meikle, Jeffrey L., *Twentieth Century Limited: Industrial Design in America, 1925–1939*, Philadelphia, Temple University Press, 1979

31) Normile, John, A.I.A., *One Story—But Three Bedrooms*, *Better Homes & Gardens*, November 1947, page 125

32) People of the State of California v. William Kesling, (transcripts), Los Angeles, March 4, 1937

33) Smith, Kyle and Nancy Smith, personal interview on February 1, 2000

34) Starr, Kevin O., *Endangered Dreams: The Great Depression in California*, New York, Oxford University Press, 1996

35) Superior Court of the State of California, *Indictments of William and Ehrma Kesling*, Los Angeles, December 8, 1936

36) Wilson, Richard, Guy et al, *The Machine Age in America 1918–1941*, New York, Harry N. Abrams, Inc, 1986

ACKNOWLEDGMENTS

I must start by thanking those who directly gave of their time and talent, beginning with my wife Julie, but closely followed by David Sadofski who worked so hard bringing his talents to so many of the photographs. Also, thanks to Jan Ipach, who recreated the floor-plans for the streamline homes from scratch and Vic Cook and Linda Hackett for their invaluable detective work and Julie Miller and Amy Quick for providing their editing talents. William Kesling's nieces Hulda Betts and Gloria Larson patiently related irreplaceable family history and other biographical information and photos from their family collection helped complete this story.

The Kesling homeowners, past and present, who were so helpful and accommodating, particularly Calhoun Chappelle, Lawrie and Joan Chisholm, Bill Christie, Bruce Ezerski, Beatrice Finley, Jean Gardner, Luis Hoyos, Toni Jones, Nadia Kaplan, Mark Kordeles, Dean Marshall, Cliff McReynolds, Robert Rang, John Rodriguez, Jane Root, Ivan Rukavina, Maddie and David Sadofski, Arne Sieg, Kyle and Nancy Smith, Sandi Sternberg, Michael Taylor, Fred Velasco, Allie Willis, and Bernard Zimmerman, all contributed to make this book possible.

Brian Cotton, Russell Forester, Lucia Forde-Murphy, Don Schmidt and John Franklin at UCLA, all supplied important information without which the book would be less complete.

Perhaps most importantly, the following few people provided continued support and encouragement and consistently offered their insight and knowledge when called upon: Denny Burt, Ann Gray, Eric Martin, Judy McKee, Ginger Moro, Philip Ethington, Pierre Koenig, and Kevin Starr at USC.

Finally, there are always people without whom a book wouldn't be possible, but without Julius Shulman this book would never have even been started. It was Julius who told me some years ago that William Kesling was a book, and it was he who made the phone call that was the first physical act leading to this book. He contributed some pretty great photographs too.
—PP